There is so much Freedom
Within!!

Love & Blessings,

Alan

12/25/09

Advance Praise for *Maximum Security: The True Meaning of Freedom*

"*Maximum Security* is the perfect book: brief, amazing, and powerful enough to change your life. Alan Gompers learned the hard way what every person on the planet needs to know – how to feel good regardless of the situation, how to be fully human, how to connect with the ultimate source of freedom. Intensely dramatic, this book takes readers on the rollercoaster of Alan Gompers' life, from the basketball courts of the Bronx to a blood-stained class room in Harlem; from the heights of Wall Street wealth to the depths of prison degradation – and then beyond, to a space that can only be described as sacred. The pages of this amazing book turn themselves. At the end, the reader is left in a state of shimmering beauty."

Stratford Sherman, co-author,
Control Your Destiny or Someone Else Will

"In *Maximum Security: The True Meaning of Freedom* Alan Gompers shows us how we imprison ourselves – and the way to regain our freedom – even if we are outside of the cement walls. True freedom comes when we finally understand that we are more than just our bodies and minds, and that God is the source of our life and strength and being. This powerful book demonstrates to us the truth: that God is within each of us, as our own true self. That is freedom indeed!"

Dr. Eugene Callender, one of America's most
prominent living civil rights leaders; friend and
associate of Dr. Martin Luther King

"I first met Alan some years ago at an 'Oldie's' concert where he was performing on stage as a personality known as 'Pop Doo-Wop.' His story is a testimony to the resiliency and greatness of the human spirit. His message is universal and important. His book, *Maximum Security: The True Meaning of Freedom*, is a rare gift to all of us. I encourage everyone to experience this amazing journey to freedom for themselves."

Rod Gilbert, NHL Hall of Fame hockey player,
New York Rangers

"All our lives we search for peace and tranquility. Some of us, like Alan, find it. It took him six years in a maximum-security prison. That's one way. Reading his book and being guided by his wisdom is a smarter way. I'm giving this book to my son."

Arthur Silver, writer & co-executive producer
of HappyDays, Laverne & Shirley, and Married
with Children (Malibu, CA)

"Alan's wonderful memoir, *Maximum Security*, is a journey of spiritual transformation that speaks to the fundamental plights of living in Western culture—insecurity, greed, and externalization. His life prior to prison was filled with success on many levels, yet Alan was plagued by a gnawing sense of unhappiness. Alone, afraid, and out of his element in prison, Alan learned to turn inward and discovered a profound stillness and wisdom. Once Alan tasted enlightenment and experienced his true Self, he devoted his life to knowing the spiritual path more fully and then sharing it with others. The love in his message is inspiring and infectious."

Dr. Michael Berman, Clinical Psychologist,
Ft. Dix Prison (New Jersey)

"*Maximum Security: The True Meaning of Freedom* is a shining example of the life-changing practice of yoga and meditation. It is the story of Alan Gompers' journey into the depths of darkness, and how, through the study and application of these ancient teachings, he found the light of true freedom. It is a wisdom-filled, inspiring testament to dedication and a touching story of redemption."

Shannon Neely, yoga instructor (Memphis, TN)

"*Maximum Security* is a clear message that we can experience freedom and happiness no matter what the situation or condition we find ourselves. A 'must read' book for anyone who seeks health, freedom and peace. In 75 years of searching, studying and teaching, few books have touched me more."

Lino Stanchich, macrobiotic teacher and author,
Power Eating Program: You Are How You Eat

"A story of a man's lust for power, the greed that drove him and how through the command of his mind, he finally discovers the road to ultimate freedom."

Don K. Reed, host of the Original Doo Wopp Shop,
WCBS-FM (New York City, NY)

"This book is surprisingly frank in regards to the feeling of being an inmate in prison. It sends a strong message to those of us who may be depressed and discouraged that there is strength in our inner self...all we have to do is summon it. Bravo!"

Raoul J. Cita, manager, writer & accompanist for
Willie Winfield and The Harptones

"*Maximum Security* will change your life. Alan Gompers' story is fascinating, exciting and without a doubt will keep you completely enthralled. Although it is one man's story about his search for peace of mind and happiness, the message is universal. Alan's story is a metaphor for the limitations and misdirections most of us experience at some time in our lives. I loved this book and recommend it to anyone who wants to experience more joy and passion in their lives."

Paul Karasik, author of *Sweet Persuasion*

"I knew Alan Gompers when he was a school teacher in the Bronx. What I didn't know was the hidden potential this beautiful man had. It took Maximum Security for Alan to discover his gifts. Through his story, we clearly see that there is a master plan and that the Universe is watching out for us. A teacher in the Bronx became a teacher who helped bond a community of faith in the prison system. I am grateful that I know Alan Gompers."

Judy Gilbert, CEO Christy MacDougall Mitchell
Advertising (New York)

"*Maximum Security* is an indelibly powerful and moving account of personal transformation under the most severe circumstances. Practicing both meditation and macrobiotics, Alan Gompers demonstrates how the power of love, peace and understanding led him to freedom and awakened in him the desire to help others. This book offers hope to anyone involved in a personal or life struggle."

Denny Waxman, macrobiotic educator
and author of *The Great Life Diet*

Maximum Security

The True Meaning of Freedom

Maximum Security

The True Meaning of Freedom

by Alan Gompers

BURNS PARK
PUBLISHERS

ANN ARBOR

(Swami) MUKTANANDA, GURUMAYI, SIDDHA YOGA and SIDDHA
MEDITATION are registered trademarks of SYDA Foundation®

ISBN: 978-0-9772286-2-1

Library of Congress Cataloging-in-Publication Data

Gompers, Alan, 1939-
  Maximum security : the true meaning of freedom / by Alan Gompers. -- 1st
ed.
     p. cm.
  Includes bibliographical references and index.
  ISBN 978-0-9772286-2-1 (alk. paper)
  1. Gompers, Alan, 1939- 2. Prisoners--United States--Biography. I. Title.

HV9468.G65 2007
365'.6092--dc22
[B]

                                                    2007022236

Manufactured in the United States of America

10 9 8 7 6 5 4 3 2 1

Dedication

To those who seek to put an end to all pain, suffering and
fear in their lives: In the end, it is fear that stands alone as the
gatekeeper to True Freedom, and it is The Mind, and only
The Mind, that attempts to incarcerate our Soul.

We are all in prison.
We are all doing time.
We all have a life sentence.
We all have a death sentence.

- Alan Gompers

Contents

Foreword

Who am I? What is the meaning of my life? Where am I going? And how, oh how, do I get there? These are life's basic questions. From time immemorial men and women have sought answers to them.

Pursuing answers to these questions takes seekers in different directions. Each individual must discover and follow his or her unique path. For some, the search will be intense, at times painful and trying. For others, it may not be their primary focus, except perhaps as death approaches. For still others, such questions may not surface at all.

Maximum Security is the fascinating story of one man's path and journey. Alan Gompers' life had once been filled with disappointment, disenchantment and seeming failure, yet he has always kept moving forward. Even a life sentence in a maximum-security prison, at first devastating, did not stop him. With Alan, as with myself, one path had to end before he could experience the radical breakthrough opening him to a whole new way of experiencing life. The illusion that he could find answers outside himself had to be given up. He had to learn to seek answers within.

Such a major shift occurs only when the time is right, an event in which we certainly play a part, but which we do not determine. One may have the good fortune, as Alan did, of eventually meeting an enlightened spiritual master, a contact that makes the journey simpler – if not always easy.

From my own lifetime of seeking and eventually finding, I urge everyone: ***Never give up!*** The answers you seek *will* be found, and your persistence is key to finding them. Your efforts *will* bear fruit. Previously unknown doors will be flung wide open, and you will bask in experiences beyond your most outrageous dreams.

Read the great odyssey of Alan's story not as an entertaining document of someone else's journey but as an instrument for contemplating your own.

Tom Toomey, South Fallsburg, New York

Tom Toomey, formerly a Catholic priest and Dominican monk for over twenty years, was the executive director of the Siddha Meditation Prison Project from 1978 to 2003. He traveled and taught all over the United States and Canada, bringing the wealth of his wisdom and his extraordinary experiences of the Siddha Yoga teachings to men and women behind prison walls.

Tom Toomey died on October 18, 2006. He will continue to be remembered with immense love and gratitude by the thousands of people whose lives he touched so deeply.

My mind is my prison.
My thoughts are my cell.
Meditation is my parole.
That's where my freedom lies.

- A meditation experience
shared by an 11 year-old boy at a
workshop with Alan Gompers.

PART I: Maximum Security

"He who fears something gives it power over him."

- Proverb

Chapter 1:

Awakening

It is a cloudless afternoon in the autumn of 1983. I am inmate #80A-2139 in Eastern New York Correctional Facility, a maximum-security prison outside Naponoch, New York.

Hundreds of inmates are out in the prison yard. The yard is huge, probably four to five acres; surrounding the whole complex is an immense concrete wall, with four equidistant gun towers on top. Some inmates, like me, stroll around in the sunshine. Others shoot hoops, lift weights, or play cards. A few groups huddle around outdoor television sets screaming obscenities as they watch a football game. A dozen or so lie on the patchy grass watching joggers circle the track. At the far end of the yard, a few guys hit softballs and run around a baseball diamond.

I find some empty bleachers where I can be alone to enjoy the beautiful weather. Climbing to the top, I sit down, close my eyes, and turn my face to the sun.

The seat vibrates beneath me. The rumbling stops, a voice breaks the stillness, and I open my eyes. An inmate is sitting a few feet away, unaware of my presence, ranting to himself. I catch the gist of what he's saying. He's going to be released in a few weeks and the first thing he plans to do is settle up with a whole lot of people who wronged him: the lawyer who misrepresented him, the judge who sentenced him, the wife who betrayed him.

His face is contorted with anger and bitterness. I can feel the waves of his negative energy as vividly as the vibrations in the bleachers under me. How can he be so unhappy when he's getting out? This guy is about to get his freedom back. Shouldn't he be more optimistic and grateful? I listen to his raving and realize that whether inside or outside, nothing will change for him. He will take his prison out into the world in the form of his rage and resentment.

I understand. For most of my life, I too have lived on an emotional roller coaster, unconscious of everything going on around me, aware only of my own dissatisfaction. We are both unwilling inhabitants of a community of a thousand men whose lives are defined by limitations and constraints. We live inside the same walls, under the same gun towers. My wife, like his, is with another man. My livelihood and money are gone. My children seem part of a different lifetime. This man is getting out in a few weeks, but I must serve thirteen more years before I even get a chance to see the parole board. There is a possibility that I will spend the rest of my life here. Under the circumstances, I could be as miserable as this guy.

And yet ...

As I sit here in these bleachers, I am happier and more at peace than I have ever been – more than I ever imagined was possible. I am aware of a profound calm emanating from deep inside me, one that brings with it a sense of joy and contentment. I am glad to be alive, grateful for the gift of a beating heart.

I have found freedom. *I have learned that true freedom flows uninterruptedly, deep inside every human being – an internal, eternal river of serenity, independent of all worldly things, available to everyone, all the time, regardless of outer circumstances.*

And I found this behind the walls of a maximum security prison.

This is my story ...

I was born in 1939, still a time of innocence and magic in New York City. My parents, Jack and Gertrude, brought me home from New York's Royal Hospital on August 16th to meet my brother Lou, seven years my senior. Home was a 5th floor apartment in Parkchester, a middle-class housing project with a population of close to 60,000 people. It still stands today, just south of Tremont Avenue on Unionport Road in the Bronx.

My great-uncle, Samuel Gompers, had immigrated to America from Holland in 1863. A tough-minded pioneer and charismatic organizer, he was the first president of the American Federation of Labor (AFL), which he co-founded in 1886. Our family took great pride in Samuel Gompers as a great American. Because of his legacy, our family was strong, politically active and civic-minded.

Like many working-class Jewish families in the 1930's, we were close. My grandparents lived nearby. Our cousins occupied the apartment above ours and my Aunt Shirley and Uncle Joe the apartment below. Friday nights our parlor was often filled with cigar smoke as the families got together to eat, play cards and discuss politics.

My mom had been raised orthodox and kept a kosher home. This meant we had to eat from two different sets of dishes so as never to mix meat and dairy. Although I had been taught that this practice was based on highly respected religious and spiritual wisdom, I didn't get it. Our orthodox practices made me feel different from the other kids.

Like the other parents, mine made me attend Hebrew school and become Bar Mitzvah'ed. I was embarrassed to be seen going to Hebrew school, and afraid to walk home afterward. Christian kids threw rocks at the synagogue, wrote hateful obscenities on the doors and the walls, and waited for us when we got out, starting fights and chasing us home.

It always seemed to me that the Jewish kids I grew up with were weaker and more afraid than the kids from the other religions, especially the Italian Catholic guys. They seemed so much more athletic and good-looking. The "fine" girls were always hanging around them. I must have run home almost every day, chased by some gang or other looking to beat me up. It didn't help that I was small and skinny as a rail.

As a child, I was plagued with upper respiratory infections, especially bronchitis. Three to four times a year, until I was a teenager, I would be stricken and run temperatures of 103 or 104 degrees. Sometimes my headaches were so bad that my mom would cry because she didn't know what to do to ease my suffering. Nobody knew what to do.

I became terrified of getting sick and dying a painful death. I became so careful about my health that I could not let myself enjoy anything at all. I was afraid fun of any kind would make me ill. This terror created my initial feelings of doubt and anger toward God. I would pray with all of my might not to get sick. But when I invariably did, I was furious at God for abandoning me in my suffering. Secretly I hoped that my anger toward God would get His attention, and make Him decide, force Him, to miraculously end my suffering. Always, I hoped and prayed for miracles.

And then, when I was eight, my mother was diagnosed with breast cancer. The doctors all promised she would return to health. I wanted to believe it for my mother's sake. But I *needed* to believe it for my own sanity and security. I needed my mom to get better for me, to feel safe in my own skin. My belief in God, my hope for my own salvation, an end to my suffering: All were entwined, inextricably dependent on my mother's full recovery.

A new procedure, called a radical mastectomy, was supposed to restore her health. She had the operation and was declared cancer-free. Her doctors said that if she had no recurrence within five years, we could assume she was cured. Months of chemotherapy and radiation followed. The surgery and drugs weakened her tremendously. She was in constant pain. For the most part, she resigned herself to her suffering. She worried that she was bothering the doctors with her complaints; my father kept trying to get the doctors to end her pain. Nothing they said or did, no matter how many visits Mom and Dad made to their offices, ever relieved her relentless, daily suffering.

After each checkup, my father would tell me there was no evidence of any spreading of the cancer. He quoted the doctors saying her pain was due to the healing process of the surgery, and was unrelated to the cancer. The operation had gotten *everything*, they assured us.

My mother was so sore that she was unable to raise her arm above her shoulder for almost a year. The doctors gave her exercises to increase her range of motion. My father put a pencil mark on the wall every time she raised her arm above the previous mark.

I remember hearing her crying and moaning in her room all the time. My mom had always been so feisty, so direct, so strong. She was the pillar of the family; her self-confidence and fearlessness had always given me strength. But after the surgery, her energy seemed to drain completely out of her. She became meek and docile. How I missed her spirit and her energy!

Five years after the surgery, seemingly still cancer-free, Mom went with Dad to Florida to celebrate their 25th wedding anniversary. They were excited about the trip and hopeful about the future. My father said the Florida sunshine would surely end her suffering. But while there in the healing sunshine, she suddenly took ill again. The cancer had returned, this time metastasizing throughout her body.

My father rushed her home. As they came through the door, his face was a mask of devastation and fear. But I was thrilled that my mother was home. She gave me a weak hug and looked at me with love. I felt relieved. Surely everything would be all right now.

Next evening, my junior-league basketball team was playing for the championship at the local community center. I couldn't think of anything but playing in that game.

But my father insisted I should stay home with my mother. Angry and frustrated, I tried to change his mind, and strong words escalated into a heated argument. My mother overheard the fight and called us into her room, which was filled with tranquility and stillness. She looked like an angel lying serenely in her bed. Her voice was so low I could hardly hear her, and she motioned us to come closer. She took my hand and reassured me that she was fine, that I should go and play basketball, and she'd see me when I got back. She looked at my father and nodded her head at him. Tears welled up in his eyes. I could see how deeply he loved her. I kissed her quickly and dashed out the door.

After the game, I couldn't wait to get home and tell everyone that we'd won. But I walked into an empty house. My mother had been rushed to the hospital while I was at the game, and the rest of the family had gone with her. A week later, she was dead. My strongest support was gone. I was thirteen, and overwhelmed with guilt and shame for having left her to play basketball. If only I had been there, been next to her, I could have somehow prevented her death.

The grief and remorse of that night never left me.

During my mom's illness I became acutely aware of a lack within me. From outside, my young life looked like it was working. My life seemed comfortable and secure. But on the inside I was tortured by incredible loneliness and confusion. I tried to mask all those horrible feelings by becoming a wild, clever, rambunctious kid who found all kinds of ways to get into trouble. I created endless ways to get attention. It became like a drug for me. Whether trying to be funny, "cute," or mischievous, I quickly discovered how to get exactly the attention I wanted.

I worked hard to be like other people, to imitate them. I learned how to copy everything about them: their words, the inflections in their voices, even their smallest movements.

I felt so inadequate in my own skin that I yearned to be anyone but me. I became envious of anyone that I believed possessed a quality I lacked. It took prodigious effort to imitate someone else. I was searching to "be" myself, but I didn't know how to do that. I didn't even know I was trying.

My first memory of personal discovery began with a

photograph I found accidentally one day. My parents usually didn't leave me on my own, but today our East Bronx apartment was all mine.

I wandered the echoing rooms of our empty apartment, looking for a distraction from the gnawing anxiety in my twelve-year old gut. Suddenly my nervousness turned to excitement. It occurred to me that this could be a great adventure! With my parents gone, I could explore all the forbidden places! I knew exactly where to begin: the "junk drawer" in my mother's antique desk in the living room. I'd had glimpses of its contents before and it seemed to be packed full of mysterious, prohibited treasures.

With a mixture of trepidation and excitement, I slid the drawer open and carefully pushed aside the stack of old snapshots on top. One black-and-white photograph slipped from the pile and fell to the floor. I retrieved it and started to put it back when something compelled me to take a closer look.

It was a faded picture of a small boy, perhaps five or six years old. He stood alone, hands in his pockets, head turned slightly downward, shoulders hunched. He looked not just shy or embarrassed, but almost ashamed to be alive. An aura of loneliness, sadness, and fear seemed to engulf him. Something about that photo kept tugging at me. Just looking at the picture made me hurt inside. What was it about this lonely little boy that hit me so hard?

Suddenly, hot tears filled my eyes. I realized that this forlorn, anonymous-looking kid in the photo was *me*. A wild, raging frustration arose in me. I could not be that kid! I did NOT want to be that kid! He was a "wimp," a "loser." He was a mirror of my father. Despite being hard working and respectable, my father was, as I saw him, a weak and beaten man. I wanted my father to be like some of the other fathers in the neighborhood, available to and interested in us kids. But he was always at work or too tired.

I had no idea what it was really like to be him, or what it was like growing up in the shadow of his parents and his family heritage. All I knew, at age 12, was that the thought of becoming like my father and experiencing life as a gentle, soft man was almost too much to handle.

The fear and insecurity that photo revealed to me that day I learned to bury deep inside. As I hurriedly put the picture away, an energy arose – a fierce new drive for outward recognition. It would become the driving force and inspiration for everything that life would ultimately bring me. From that moment on, I burned to be in absolute control of my life.

Chapter 2:

"The West"

Parkchester, where I grew up, was home to mostly middle-class Jewish, Italian, and Irish New Yorkers. It was divided into four quadrants: North, East, South and West. The quadrants not only defined where we lived, but determined the schools we attended. Parkchester was a self-contained city within a city. There were supermarkets, parks, playgrounds, movie theaters, huge parking garages, department stores, and schools. We even had our own police force and maintenance crew. I lived in the West quadrant and spent most of the first twenty years of my life "hanging out at The West," as we called it.

In "The West," as in the other quadrants, every kid was measured by his ability on the basketball court. Nobody cared much about what he did off the court. The best players got the most respect.

I figured there were two ways to get the kind of respect and admiration I desired. One way was to put in the effort to become a great player; the other was to become friends with a great player, let his status rub off on me and get the recognition that way. So I went out of my way to become friends with the best players.

At the same time I also tried to develop my game, but I never practiced hard enough to get really good. But on the court, in a game, I wanted to win so bad, to impress everyone watching so much, that I became driven. I was so competitive that I couldn't walk away without having left everything I had out on the court.

On those basketball courts of The West I discovered the mind-blowing high of victory. I became addicted to its ecstatic rush. Oh, how I loved to win! It gave me an all-consuming feeling of worthiness and satisfaction.

Music was another passion. I started playing saxophone when I was about eight. My teacher was my Uncle Joe, who lived one flight below us. He'd been a professional musician and bandleader with the famous Vincent Lopez orchestras of the 30's and 40's that played on the big luxury ocean liners. My uncle would come up to my apartment with his tenor sax and accompany me on my alto. He taught me the techniques of the professional musician.

My father and Uncle Joe wanted me to develop my musical talent by attending the High School for Music and Art in New York City. My friends from Parkchester were all going to James

Monroe High School in the Bronx. Initially, I felt totally left out and alone. I didn't want to travel all the way to Manhattan where I didn't know anyone; I wanted to stay in my neighborhood with my friends from The West.

Music and Art required auditions and written tests for prospective students to be accepted. Most of the kids who went there had training in classical music, and most of them played instruments of a symphony orchestra. The saxophone wasn't a classical instrument. It was used in dance bands or jazz combos. I didn't think playing sax gave me much chance of getting into such a prestigious school. My uncle, however, had an extraordinary idea: Why not surprise them with a familiar classical piece played on an unconventional instrument? So he wrote an intricate arrangement for the saxophone of Brahms' Hungarian Dance No. 5.

The day of the audition I stood in front of a panel of five starchy-looking people with serious, unfriendly faces. Determined to show them what I could do, I played my Uncle's arrangement and didn't look up until I was done. I was astonished to see that they were smiling, radiating approval. They gave me a standing ovation! A few weeks later I received my acceptance letter, a triumph for my uncle, my father, and me.

Then came Doo-Wop – the birth of rock 'n' roll, the sound of the 50's. If the 20's had been made for my father, the 50's were made for me. Doo-Wop was *my* music and this music brought me to life!

I discovered this sound late one night walking around my neighborhood. The streets were empty and everything was still. I turned a corner and saw five guys standing on the sidewalk, harmonizing together. The song was "A Sunday Kind of Love," a slow, soulful ballad. As I listened to the deep, evocative harmony, I thought my heart would fall out of my chest. The sound was so indescribably sweet, so rich and beautiful that it filled my eyes with tears. That night I experienced the fullness of my heart. Maybe for the first time in my life, I fell in love.

I was immediately convinced that somehow this music would help me find the happiness I ached for so desperately. Doo-Wop became my hope, my inspiration.

After that night, Doo-Wop seemed to show up everywhere. Singing groups appeared under streetlamps, on park benches, in hallways, school bathrooms, subway platforms – anywhere there was an echo to amplify the sound and deepen the harmony. Forming my own group was inevitable.

Many Doo-Wop groups named themselves after cars: The Impalas, The Cadillacs, The Skylarks, The Montereys, The Jaguars. Four friends from school and I formed an *a cappella* group. We called ourselves The Montclairs, after my brother Lou's first car. And Doo-Wop truly was a vehicle. The first song we harmonized together was "A Sunday Kind of Love." It was recorded originally by a legendary group from the 50's featuring one of the great voices from our era, "Willie Winfield and The Harptones." We sang because it made us feel happy, united. Doo-Wop transported us into a state of outrageous joy. To this day,

I still get goose bumps whenever I listen to any of the legendary groups of the 50's.

The Montclairs gained success doing gigs and even, after a short time, making records. As one of the singers of the group I got more attention. I began to taste the awesome, intoxicating magic of fame and fortune. I became ecstatic when people applauded my singing; I couldn't get enough.

As a teenager, I thought I had it all. I had name – they called me "The Gomp." I had game – basketball, the only game that mattered growing up in the Bronx. And I had music – Doo-Wop! It didn't get any better than that!

After high school, I tried to keep The Montclairs together but the guys went their own ways. One joined the army. Our lead singer went out West to become a movie star and recorded a song I wrote, "My Dreams Have Gone." He appeared in the movie *The Big Fisherman* with John Saxon, and then he dropped out of sight. For a short time, the remaining three of us got together with some other guys and tried to recreate the group, but once I went off to college, The Montclairs dissolved for good.

Chapter 3:

Ramona

College was my father's idea. He wanted for me what he never had for himself. Continually prodding me to consider my future, my father insisted that nothing was as important as education. He knew I, unlike himself, had a chance to make something of my life. I should stay in school and go to college.

In 1957 I enrolled at Hunter College in the Bronx. My grade point average wasn't high enough to admit me as a full-time student, so I drove a truck during the day and went to classes at night. Getting into day school a year later was the fulfillment of my father's dreams for me. He wanted me to have a secure future, and believed that becoming a teacher would give me respect and dignity.

I loved campus life. I dove for the swimming team. On the newly formed wrestling team, I won the first match in Hunter College history and went undefeated in my first full season. I played varsity baseball for two years as a pitcher and an outfielder. I pole-vaulted for the track team until one day, barefoot, I landed outside the sawdust pit and nearly killed myself. I was also good at gymnastics and enjoyed the trampoline.

Not surprisingly, the idea of becoming a physical education teacher and coach appealed to me. What I liked even more was the prospect of a job that would allow me to stay in shape, not require too much classroom time, and provide holidays and summers off.

I chose easy courses with professors who were known to grade leniently, and played sports as much as possible. I graduated with a degree in Health and Physical Education and couldn't wait to get started teaching. PE teaching jobs were the "sweetest" in the system. I took a test and ranked seventh out of 300, but there were no vacancies in the entire city. So I became a substitute teacher, and later taught science full-time at a junior high at 138th Street and Lenox Avenue, in the center of Harlem.

The year was 1962. The Black Panthers and the Five-Percenters, a radical Black Muslim group, had become a volatile presence in Harlem. It was not a safe place for whites, Jews, or cops; I had two strikes against me. Not even the schools were safe. Because of the robbers, pimps, and gangsters who routinely broke in, women were barred from teaching in ground-floor classrooms.

I was given a key to the science lab with strict, specific instructions: First, lock the door from the inside as soon as all the kids are in the room, then pull down the window shades. When the bell rings at the end of the period, have the kids line up at the door and make them wait while I open the shade, check the hall for safety, and only then open the door. After the students left the room, lock the door again until the next class was lined up in the hall. I repeated this procedure for each and every class.

Yet, even though I wasn't thrilled about being locked in a classroom all day, I really liked my job. The kids were a challenge, sure, but I respected the difficult issues they faced each day of their young lives. They were tough and angry, but I loved them. I tried hard to treat them as I would have liked to have been treated at their age – with dignity and respect.

I was amazed how hard *they* tried to make the best of their terrible circumstances. We once started a unit on the internal combustion engine. I asked my eighth-grade class to look around their neighborhoods for discarded auto parts to bring to school. Rather than finding old parts at home, they "found" some "new" parts for their assignment. By the end of the week, my classroom looked like a NAPA warehouse, with a variety of brand-new auto parts in their original boxes.

For my first open-school night, I told my students that I wanted their parents to come and meet me. One kid, a good boy who missed a lot of school but wasn't a discipline problem, showed up with a raggedy derelict whom he introduced as his father. The guy wasn't exactly drunk, but he was dirty and incoherent. I took the boy aside and quietly asked if this was really his father. He looked at me with sad eyes and said, "I don't have no mother or father, Mr. G. I don't have no home, either. I sleep in the park every night. This is one of the guys I know from the park. I didn't want to disappoint you by not bringing anyone to open-school night." Sometime after that, he stopped coming to school. I found out later that he was still living in the park, getting high and running the streets.

Six months later, I was offered a job at Columbus High School in the Bronx teaching P.E., Math, and English. I jumped at the chance. Although I had no idea how to teach Math or English, I thought this would give me a foot in the door for a full-time P.E. job later on.

After I left, the teacher who took over my class was a young, arrogant guy who thought he was tough because he was big. He learned firsthand the danger of not respecting those "street" kids. One morning shortly after I'd left, school officials found him half dead on the floor of the science lab, bleeding from nearly 30 stab wounds. He spent months in the hospital recuperating.

Eventually I got the full-time P.E. job I wanted at Taft High School in the Bronx. A few years later I transferred to James Monroe, the school assigned to residents of Parkchester who lived in the West quadrant; it was where I would have gone if I hadn't been accepted into Music & Art. Back in the Bronx, I felt I was home.

Soon after I graduated college, I married a pretty girl named Lynn Bader. I met and fell in love with her at her Sweet Sixteen party, where I'd been hired to sing with the Montclairs. She was dating someone else, but like so many girls, she became infatuated with one of the singers in the group: in this case, me.

We married when she was 19 and I was 22. A year later, our baby Gina was born. For the first time in my life, I thought I'd finally found real meaning and direction. I had everything I wanted: a family, a job, and people who loved me.

Unfortunately, it didn't last long. Shortly after Gina was born, our marriage began to disintegrate. We had married for all the wrong reasons. Lynn married me because she hated her parents and wanted desperately to get out of their house. I married her because I was lonely and wanted someone to fill the hole in my heart. Lynn was beautiful and sexy, and she wanted to marry me. What else did I need? That was about the depth of my values at the time.

After a short time, I knew I wanted to end our marriage, but I was terrified of being alone in the world. My life as a young father and husband was a living hell, but the thought of being alone was even worse. I wasn't courageous enough to leave, so Lynn did. I tried desperately to stop her, even as I felt the need to break loose and be free. She reassured me it would be a trial separation, just for a few weeks. Part of me wanted to believe that, but at a deeper level, I knew it was the end.

Just a year and a half after our wedding, I drove her, her mother, and the baby to the airport to see them off to Los Angeles. Lynn had family in California. As Lynn and Gina boarded their plane, I was overcome by anguish at losing my daughter. One minute she had been in my arms and the next she was gone. I gazed out the smudged airport window over the bleak runway as the plane began to taxi. I scanned the tiny portholes, one by one, looking for their faces. As the plane lifted off and disappeared, a part of me died.

Lynn knew a guy in LA who was originally from New York, a wealthy, successful businessman who had been madly in love with her for years. He and I had played on the Hunter College baseball team together, and oddly enough, his name was Alan, too. Within a year, our divorce was final and they were married.

Now I could hardly find a reason to get up in the morning. Going to work every day, facing the kids at school, was all exhausting. At the end of the day I just wanted to go home, crawl into bed, and shut off my mind. But staying in the house day after day became even more depressing. I was afraid to go out, and depressed by being homebound. Once again, I was stuck, feeling imprisoned by my negative emotions.

And then, suddenly and mysteriously, that dynamic force inside me took over. The raging energy that had risen in me as a twelve-year-old boy snooping in his mother's desk drawer came alive in me again at age 25. This inner force, longing for an outlet, led me to graduate school.

In the fall of 1964, I enrolled in Hunter College Graduate School in the Masters program for Health and Physical Education. I attended classes four nights a week and continued to teach during the day. I always felt better when I forced myself to leave my room.

One night at the start of the semester, I wandered into the student lounge between classes and spotted two guys I'd grown up with in my neighborhood. Marty was from the South Bronx. Although we didn't know each other well, we'd been opponents in a basketball league at the 92nd Street "Y" in midtown Manhattan. Marty was laid back, easy to be with, outrageously funny without trying. Stewie, a few years younger than me, had also grown up in Parkchester. At six-two, he was a big guy who played basketball for Columbus High School and then later on for Hunter College, both in the Bronx. Because of our age difference we'd grown up hanging out with different crowds.

In the student lounge that night, I looked over at them laughing and carrying on. They recognized me and called me over. I didn't feel much like talking to anyone, but taken off guard by their friendliness, I found myself walking over. They welcomed me like we'd been friends for years, and immediately made me feel comfortable.

Stewie also taught P.E. in the Bronx. That first night in the student lounge, he did most of the talking. He was a character, always "on," seeming never to take life seriously. He said the most outrageous and amazing things. I'd never met anyone so carefree. Once he had me laughing so hard that I was almost crying. It was great to feel alive again.

Hanging out, reminiscing about playing ball and the girls we knew, I felt a sense of belonging and security I hadn't felt in a long time. After that night, the three of us took every chance we got to tour the playgrounds of the Bronx, challenging anyone to beat us at basketball. It was rare that anyone did.

My rekindled friendship with Marty was short-lived, however.

Marty had an addiction to Orange Julius, a frothy, malty orange juice drink that was the rage at the time. He made a ritual of having an Orange Julius after every basketball game. When he heard that the company was closing its New York stores, he decided there was nothing left for him on the east coast. In California, Orange Julius was still alive and well. And so Marty left, lured by a drink and the promise of warm weather.

My friendship with Stewie thrived, and we became inseparable. We went to parties all over town. Almost daily we played basketball one-on-one, establishing a ritual of intense competition. We tried to outdo each other in every aspect of our lives, even competing in the selection of restaurants. One week Stewie would find an eatery, and because he'd found it first, I felt compelled to find a better one the next week. Then we'd argue about whose restaurant was superior.

Above all, Stewie made me laugh. I never saw him serious about anything. If I even hinted at getting down on myself, he'd call me "Sorry Al," which I hated. To make it even worse, he would burst into hysterical laughter. My hatred of being called "Sorry Al" taught me how to mask my emotional state. I learned how to change it instantly, almost effortlessly, simply by willing it. I used this ability automatically just to avoid Stewie's teasing.

As much as I enjoyed teaching, I was getting restless. Spending the rest of my life doing the same thing and making so little money sounded like a prison sentence, and I wanted to break out!

One afternoon in the spring of 1968, as I headed into the boys' gym at Monroe High, I ran into a group of other male P.E.

teachers gossiping outside the office. Apparently a gorgeous new secretary had started working that day. Acting like high school kids themselves, the gym teachers were taking turns strolling casually into the office to check her out. I decided it was my turn.

I had never seen so many people there at one time. Once I got a peek at the new girl, it was easy to see why the place was jammed. She was not only beautiful, but she had a presence that was intensely, disturbingly sensual. I found it hard to stay in the room. Her long black hair fell to her waist, smooth and full of light. Her lips were full and moist, breathtakingly soft-looking. She had high, subtly defined cheekbones, huge black eyes, and rich brown skin.

As I stood there trying not to gape, she got up and walked over to a file cabinet. I thought all the men would pass out. The room filled with moans and sighs, yet she seemed completely unaware of her effect on us; her focus was on her job. Of course, this gave her an even greater sense of mystery and allure.

Ramona Lopez-Colon was almost nineteen, ten years younger than me, and she took my breath away. We didn't start dating until she graduated high school, and then I went after her with such blind, intense passion that she never had a chance to say "no." I finally convinced her to move in with me. Over dinner one evening, I proposed and Ramona accepted. Her family welcomed the news – and me – with warmth and joy. I was thrilled to find love again, the kind of love that my parents had shared.

I once asked my father how he met my mom. His face lit up.

He met her at a dance parlor in Coney Island. My dad always said that he picked her not just because she was a "looker," but because she also knew how to dance. They grew up during the Roaring 20's when ballroom dancing had reached a glorious crescendo. Dances like "The Black Bottom," "The Charleston," and "The Peabody" captured the hearts of all of America.

As a kid, I loved watching my father dance, especially with his sister, my Aunt Shirley, who lived one flight below us. If there was one thing my father loved more than anything else, it was dancing. It was his way of letting go, releasing his inhibitions, and feeling free.

My wedding to Ramona was spectacular, one of the most extraordinary days of my life. Ramona never looked more beautiful. The ceremony was held at Temple Addath Israel, the second largest synagogue in New York. Although I certainly didn't consider myself a practicing Jew, the wedding was really my way of honoring my beautiful mother. Although Ramona had been raised Catholic, she converted to Judaism. In her mind, it was important that our future children be raised with one faith.

The reception hall was filled with tables of food and rows of people. On one side sat my Jewish family, on the other, Ramona's Puerto Rican relatives. The two halves remained divided until the music started. As soon as the band began to play a Mambo, my father walked over to Ramona's family, picked out the first beautiful young Spanish girl he could find, and asked her to dance. The happiness and joy he found in dancing brought our wedding reception to life and united our two families.

Chapter 4:

Winnie

One day in the fall of 1966, Stewie told me he'd found a great way for us to make money. A history teacher in his school owned a small investment company on the side, and the guy had offered Stewie and me jobs selling mutual funds.

Winnie Marucci had been a wrestler in the circuses and carnivals of the 30's and 40's. He had cauliflower ears and was built like a Sumo wrestler – about five-foot four and 300 pounds. He was the strongest human being I'd ever met, although nothing about him was threatening, for he was incredibly gentle. Once I saw him lift a full-size refrigerator and carry it on his back up a flight of stairs. This was at a community center called The Bronx House, where he was the after-school athletic director. Stewie and I went to visit him one day to talk about the mutual fund business, and someone asked him if he could help move a refrigerator that was blocking an entrance. "Of course," Winnie said.

Stewie and I tagged along. The refrigerator was parked in front of a staircase. Winnie backed up to the appliance, squatted down, bent over slightly, and grabbed the refrigerator from behind. He tilted it forward to a 45-degree angle, got his back underneath it, and to our amazement, walked it up a full flight of stairs – with a landing halfway up, no less. Then he trotted back downstairs and resumed the conversation where we had left off.

Winnie said that when he was a wrestler, the ring announcer would dare the audience to wrestle him for a $500 cash prize – in those days and in those towns, a small fortune. Many tried, to no avail. On the few occasions Winnie found himself in danger of losing, he'd maneuver his challenger over to a strategically placed curtain where a crony hid out with a lead pipe to ensure the outcome.

After his carnival days he became a professional boxer. He said that after he won his first eight or nine fights by knockout, he began to think he couldn't be beat. But then he came up against a young black fighter who was so fast and strong that Winnie couldn't see the punches coming. Five rounds of the worst beating he'd ever taken finally enraged him, and the carnival wrestler in him took over. When the bell rang for the sixth round, Winnie ran to his opponent's corner, grabbed him, lifted him high over his head, and threw him into the crowd.

He was disqualified, of course. He said he lost the fight and also his desire ever to wear boxing gloves again. Teaching was much easier, and the investment company, Westchester

Investor's Service, provided a challenge and some extra cash.

Now, I'd never sold anything in my life, but Stewie made it sound easy. He was like a man possessed, and so excited he almost foamed at the mouth. The thought of making money, real money, enough to be rich, just about took him out of his skin.

"We can do this!" he said. "We can make a fortune. Between the two of us, we can sell anything to anyone. No one can sell like me and you!"

I thought he was crazy.

I would come to understand two things about Stewie: He was extremely creative and perceptive, and he was totally mercenary. He would have done just about anything, given enough money. He once told me he would get down on his hands and knees and push a penny with his nose across a room filled with human excrement if there was a high enough stack of greenbacks on the other side. To Stewie, money was God, and I got swept up into this insanity right along with him.

We took the test to qualify as Registered Representatives licensed to sell stocks and mutual funds. We became partners. I began by selling mutual funds to the teachers and staff at my school. To my surprise, it was easy. Stewie was right: I had a gift for getting people to do what I wanted. True to our pattern, Stewie and I met each day after school to see who had made more sales that day. It soon became so competitive that I wouldn't leave school until I had gotten enough new deals to make sure that I had Stewie beat.

I was so turned on by this new career that I came home every day with a shopping bag full of new orders. When I ran out of teachers, I began calling everyone in my address book: friends, family, my doctor, dentist, plumber, and anyone else I could think of. I made sure that everyone I sold referred me to their friends, which provided an unending supply of new prospects. The more money I made, the more driven I became. In the first two months, I made more money than I had made the whole year teaching. I got high off the money, my increasing confidence, and power. People began to notice me and treat me with respect. I could hardly contain myself, certain I'd at last found success. Money could get me whatever I wanted in life, and now I knew how to get it.

Our arrangement with Winnie was typical for new salesmen. We were paid a portion of the commission on everything we sold – 60 percent for Winnie and 40 percent for us, which Stewie and I divided. But as we became successful, we began to hound Winnie to sweeten our end of the deal. After eight months he caved in to our pressure and made us full partners, and we began splitting the commissions equally.

Stewie and I wanted no part of the paperwork and administrative stuff, so Winnie gradually took on that responsibility entirely. Of course, that didn't leave him much time to sell, which made it easy for us to start thinking he wasn't holding up his end. We stopped seeing his contribution as important and began to measure his value solely on his sales record. As the business grew, we outsold Winnie every month. He was becoming an obstacle to our success.

Since we had little experience in the financial community and nowhere else to go, at first we resigned ourselves to the situation. But we grew increasingly impatient, frustrated, and critical of Winnie's every move. We prodded him and poked fun at his "ineptitude" as a salesman. For his part, Winnie was so gentle and good-natured that he didn't take any of our abuse seriously.

In the spring of 1967, Westchester Investor's Service came to the attention of a Wall Street investment banking and brokerage firm, North American Planning Corporation. They'd noticed we were breaking sales records with Oppenheimer, Dreyfus and Fidelity Mutual Funds, and they wanted us to come in as sales managers and develop a sales team. They offered a package that included a salary and much higher commissions, plus bonuses and overrides on whatever our salesmen brought in. They said we could make three times what we made as teachers, maybe more.

Neither of us had ever sold a stock before. I wasn't sure I even knew what a stock was. Whatever they were, I knew I could sell them. I was convinced that success came not from selling a product, but from figuring out the client. I remained confident in spite of my ignorance. Little did I realize how much this approach – blissful ignorance combined with a willingness to manipulate others – would come back to haunt me.

Stewie and I decided to use the approaching summer break to give ourselves completely to this stock venture. But Winnie was very much against this idea. He felt we had a good thing by ourselves, and that we controlled our own destiny by being independent business owners. He didn't want to work for anyone else, and he didn't trust the people from North American Planning Corporation. They were too sharp and fast-talking, he said. Stewie and I jumped all over him, and in the end he reluctantly gave in.

Stewie and I dove full blast into our new environment. We now had real offices in the heart of midtown Manhattan, in the Pan American building at 40th Street and Park Avenue, just down the street from the Waldorf Astoria. We had desks and phones and enough expense money to advertise for new sales reps for the team we were putting together. We placed ads in the *New York Times* and in the newsletter of the United Federation of Teachers. We figured that if *we* teachers could do it, others could too. Eventually, two or three who signed on became full-time, successful brokers.

About six months after we started with North American Planning Corporation, the General Manager called us into his office. He said he thought we were great salesmen and potentially dynamic leaders. He wanted us to become managers. We were ecstatic. This was exactly what we were hoping for: We were on our way! We would have our own offices, bigger commissions, and the opportunity to move up with the company.

But what about Winnie? The GM said Winnie was welcome to stay on as a salesman but not as a manager. That was okay with us. Winnie, we told each other, didn't have our sales power or our commitment. He would be fine as a salesman; meanwhile,

Stewie and I were destined for great things. We could not have cared less about Winnie, except that we needed to figure out how to tell him.

We need not have been concerned. As we sat in our new office wondering how to break the news, and contemplating our expected meteoric rise, the door flew open and Winnie came thundering in. Before either of us could say a word, he put his head down like a bull and charged. He grabbed us both by our shirts and ties, lifted us off the ground, and pinned us against the wall. We gaped helplessly at this short, crazed gorilla and thought our lives were about to end. He held us for about ten seconds. Then he let us drop and let out a deafening, terrifying, inhuman roar. He punched the radiator, which folded like an accordion and fell to the floor, leaving a hole in the wall.

Stewie and I stared at him and he stared back, chest heaving. I didn't breathe for fear of setting him off again. Gradually he calmed down. Tears welled in his eyes and spilled down his cheeks. He continued to stare at us and finally said, "What did I ever do to make you want to hurt me?"

Shaken and speechless, Stewie and I just looked at him. There was nothing to say. Wiping his eyes and shaking his head, Winnie turned and walked out the door. The crowd that had gathered outside our office parted, and he left in silence. My heart broke. It was the last time he ever spoke to us.

Chapter 5:

New Issues

A few days later we had all but forgotten the incident. Our path was now free of obstacles, and all we thought about was charging ahead. The skies opened up and heaven began to rain money upon us.

One of the more experienced sales managers at North American Planning Corporation was an old-time, cigar-chomping con man named Jules Levy. This guy was outrageous; nothing about him was real. He was like the old stand-up vaudeville comics; his golden-brown toupee didn't come close to matching, or covering, the few gray hairs remaining on his head. He talked out of the side of his mouth, as if conveying a juicy secret. Leaning forward, he'd look from side to side to make sure no one was eavesdropping, then whisper his cigar breath into your ear.

The rest of the staff knew enough about the business to recognize Jules for what he was – a deceitful scoundrel about to be axed within a few months – and they ignored him. But

Stewie and I were flattered by his attention. Jules knew we were out of our depth in the corporate world. We thought he could give us inside information that would make us rich. He used his comical appearance to disarm and manipulate us. Before he'd talk business he'd get us laughing, and we inevitably wound up doing whatever he wanted without looking too closely at the details or thinking about the consequences. Because he made it all sound so exciting – and legitimate – we never wanted to scrutinize the illegal things he got us to do.

One morning Jules called us into his office and told us about "new issues." A new issue, he explained, is a stock that's about to be traded publicly for the first time. People could buy new issue stock without paying a commission, and they'd also have the "privilege" of getting it before the general public. The stock market works on the principle of supply and demand. If more people bought a stock than sold it, he explained, the stock rose in price. The trick was to have more people buying than selling. Then everyone would be "guaranteed" to make money.

Jules's new issue was an offering for 100,000 shares at three dollars a share in an Italian frozen-food company called Rotonelli Foods. It was being made available only to special clients of the firm, but because we were new to the business and he wanted to help us, he'd give us the opportunity to get our clients in on it. He advised us to urge our clients to hold their shares until we told them to sell.

New issues are perfectly legal. The participating brokerage houses usually acquire most of the stock and offer it first to their best customers at what's called an "underwriting price." If the hype and the publicity make a new issue desirable, it becomes a "hot issue." A hot issue will generally open to the public at a premium price because the hype has created an active "after market." This means buyers who couldn't get the stock at the underwriting price, and who think it will rise in value, will line up to buy it as soon as it goes public. This creates a "short" in the trader's inventory: he has sold more stock than he owns. Under SEC regulations, he must deliver this stock within five business or seven calendar days. To cover the short in his inventory, the broker raises the market price of the stock to induce owners to sell. He will continue to raise the price until someone sells, because if no one sells in time for him to meet the SEC deadline, he will be forced to buy it himself at a higher price than he sold it.

It's all legal, but it's a dangerous game if you don't know what you're doing. You need a lot of starch in your underwear to play. If you are a broker with a larcenous bent, it can be tempting to remove some of the risk by controlling the market. You tell your customers to hold onto their stock, then wait as the company trader raises the price. At the last minute, when the price is at a nice juicy level, you dump all your stock and, by the way, take a huge profit. Only then do you tell the other stockowners to sell. If your customers trust you enough to sign a discretionary power of attorney to buy and sell for them, even better: You can do it all without their knowledge. Usually this results in a collapse in the stock's market price.

This is not the free trading market regulated by "fair and orderly" buying and selling, which the SEC promotes; it is totally controlled and manipulated by an individual or group for their own profit. The SEC takes a dim view of such practices. And this was precisely what our friend Jules was up to.

He knew Rotonelli would open at a premium. He bought the underwriting stock for himself under an assumed name – that in itself is a felony – and then got idiots like Stewie and me to sell it to our customers and tell them to hold it until we gave them the word. This is a practice, Stewie and I later learned, common in small firms and large.

Stewie and I were skeptical and thought it sounded too good to be true. Then Jules uttered the word "guaranteed." Those magic syllables switched a light on in me (security!) and I felt like I'd struck gold. Stewie and I exchanged sly smiles, and in that moment we were hooked. Part of me knew this was sleazy. But I had entered a fantasy world of such intense promise that I turned my back on reality. I found ways to rationalize what was happening and I was in complete denial.

We offered our clients the new issue, which went public a few months later. Within a week it jumped from three to six dollars a share. By then, having doubled our clients' money, we were allowed to take them out of the stock. Stewie and I were blown away. It was like New Year's Eve. We jumped up and down like lunatics. And it was all so simple. It was guaranteed! We were told we couldn't lose, and we didn't.

Of course our clients were all very grateful and eagerly

anticipated the next investment opportunity. In most cases, they were, on a different level, doing exactly what we were doing – turning a blind eye to reality and getting caught up in the excitement. After all, wasn't making tons of money the name of the game? Maybe it wasn't completely on the up-and-up, but when I looked around, it seemed that everyone was playing the same way. Why hadn't anyone else thought of this? All those professional investment analysts seemed like fools! They spent all that money and time in school learning economics and the intricacies of the investment world, and we walk in, two lowly gym teachers with no financial training, and immediately outperform the so-called geniuses of the industry. Oh, we had it all figured out! Everyone was blind. We had unlocked the Secret of the Universe, all by ourselves. Needless to say, as our profits soared, so did our egos.

Stewie and I sat brainstorming one day, looking for new ways to develop our client base. We came up with the idea of going up to New York's Catskill Mountains – the "Borscht Belt" – and offering free stock-market lectures at the hotels. We would give our little lecture, then reveal the name and price of our stock pick of the week. We'd promise that the price would increase during the coming week and go so far as to quote it to them. You don't have to buy anything, we'd say; simply watch the price as the week unfolds.

I still had my contacts from summer jobs in college, and my idea immediately went over with them. The hotel owners loved it; it didn't cost them a thing, yet provided a free activity for the guests. We were given meeting rooms, microphones, and refreshments to offer the guests, all *gratis*.

Our first lecture was a bit unsettling, since no one who showed up seemed to be under eighty years old. Some of the women fell asleep over their knitting. Many of the men dozed off too, and we wondered if we could be heard over their snoring. The scene would have been hilarious if we weren't so serious. We merely shrugged, rolled our eyes, and tried not to let it bother us.

The following week we returned. Sure enough, the price had increased to the exact figure we'd projected. We actually had discussed with the trader how much stock he required us to buy in order for the price to go up as much as we wanted. The trader would tell us what he needed – let's say 5,000 shares – to move the stock one point. Stewie and I would tell him to move the stock up one point on the day we went to the mountains; we guaranteed that we'd get enough orders to fill the 5,000 shares. Of course we were on the hook for it if we couldn't fill the orders, but we knew we could. And we did! We convinced customers and their referrals to invest by promising them stock in the next hot new issue. We also got orders from a few of the new salesmen. After a while, we simply told the trader what price to make the stock and he was satisfied we'd make it happen.

Gradually more and more people became excited. It was as though we were divulging the winner before a race started. New clients were attracted all the time, giving us ever-increasing buying power, which in turn gave us even more control of stock prices. We always chose companies with a limited amount of stock available for purchase so that just a little buying and selling changed the price. We cultivated a small group of investors who gave us power of attorney and built up enough buying power to manipulate the price any way we wanted. The power was awesome. I began to feel invincible, an illusion supported by the adulation of other brokers and employees in the company.

Chapter 6:

Sweet Revenge

Even while Stewie and I were selling so successfully, we were still teaching full time. In spite of our success, we didn't want to give up the security of our jobs. At the end of the summer of 1969, just days after my 30th birthday, we finally decided to take a leave of absence from our first careers because work was going so well with North American Planning Corporation and we couldn't see stopping now.

That winter, a company called Lincoln Securities made us a very attractive offer. It included a generous override on everything our salesmen produced, and top commission on all that we produced with our own customers. They would give us a fifty-fifty split, after expenses, on everything we sold on our end – Stewie, myself and our sales team. I didn't quite understand what expenses they were talking about, and that made me uncomfortable, but Stewie convinced me not to worry because the deal overall was very sweet. We signed on, and Lincoln

Securities set us up in a new office in the Pelham Parkway section of the Bronx.

Billy and Richie, the company owners, introduced us to a few other stocks they'd been trading, some of which came from a firm called Mark Serrano & Company. They convinced us that we should diversify and that our salesmen and customers should be involved in more than one stock at a time. It wasn't long before Stewie and I both began to suspect we weren't getting all our money. Billy and Richie evaded our questions. Months passed and things got worse. We figured they owed us about $25,000 each, a small fortune when you consider that teachers at that time lived on $100 a week. They were lying for sure. We knew they were stealing but couldn't figure out how they were doing it. Each time we confronted them we were met with vehement denial, and the meeting always ended in a shouting match. They double-talked their way out, always managing to make it look like we had it all wrong. Even when Stewie and I threatened to leave and take our sales crew with us, they weren't fazed.

It got to the point where I didn't even want to be in the same room with them. Our vision of a great opportunity had deteriorated into a nightmare. We got more angry and frustrated every day, until we eventually decided to get some help, some explanation and direction. Mark Serrano, whom we'd met months before, seemed trustworthy, so we called him to set up a meeting.

In Mark's office we told him our story and he confirmed our suspicions. Mark explained how they were getting over on us and what we needed to do to get them to settle up. I told Stewie I wasn't going through another one of those frustrating shouting matches with them again. I believed that no matter what we said, regardless of how we presented it, they would find a way to twist it to make it seem like they didn't owe us anything. I felt we needed stronger action.

One of us said we ought to scare the money out of them and we laughed. I said I knew the perfect guy for the job: Bernard Orr, a security guard at James Monroe High School, who stood six-four and weighed about 240. We used to play basketball together.

"Yeah," Stewie said, getting into it. "Bernie and Eddie Smalls!"

Eddie Smalls was a professional prizefighter who lived in Stewie's apartment building. He loved Stewie and was always showing up at his apartment. A year before, he had been mugged by a gang who beat him with bats and metal pipes, then cut his face with a razor and left him for dead. His face was so disfigured by scar tissue that he looked like a real-life monster. The lower lid of one eye had been cut away, and it looked as if his eyeball was going to fall out of the socket, especially when he got angry. Bernie and Eddie: the perfect duo. We looked at each other, grinning.

I spoke to Bernie, and Stewie approached Eddie. We stressed that we didn't want them to hurt Billy and Richie, just scare them. We figured their appearance alone probably would be enough. We would set up a meeting with Billy and Richie, and

Eddie and Bernie would break in on it. Eddie and Bernie thought the whole idea sounded like fun. We offered them money but they wouldn't accept it, although they did agree to let us take them out to dinner afterwards to celebrate. Then we called Mark and told him what we were up to. He loved it; as far as he was concerned, Billy and Richie were two cowards getting what they deserved. Mark told us he had always felt they were up to no good because they always called us "the two idiot gym teachers from the Bronx" who were going to make them rich. This made my blood boil.

Before we hung up, Mark suggested we hold the meeting at his office so they wouldn't suspect anything. And after the meeting we should sit down together and discuss the possibility of moving our operation over to his company. He'd work out a solid deal, he said, one that would make us a lot of money. When I heard that, I knew everything would unfold perfectly.

So Stewie and I met with Billy and Richie. We opened with the old complaint that we didn't think we were getting all our money. Billy immediately jumped up. "Is this the reason you brought us down here, to go over the same old nonsense again?" he roared. "You've been paid all your money. You're not getting another dime from us!"

Right on cue, Bernie and Eddie walked in. The look on Eddie's face was so intense that I began to worry. A scowling Bernie moved in close, towering over everyone. The room fell silent.

Billy recovered first, yelling that he was not going to be

threatened by "a couple of goons." Eddie's face reddened and contorted in rage. He grabbed the enormously overweight Richie by his shirtfront and dragged him to the window. He grabbed his tie and cursed, swinging him from side to side. "So you're not going to pay them what you owe?" he yelled.

Terrified, Richie shrieked, "We will, we will! We'll do anything you want!"

But Eddie did not seem to be mollified. He held Richie against the wall with one hand and with the other, yanked the window open from the bottom. He pushed Richie over to it and pulled his head down, as if he was about to throw him out from the 24th floor. Richie begged for his life. "Please don't do this. We're sorry! We'll pay them all the money we took. It's all our fault. We were wrong." He began to weep. "Please don't hurt me, I have a family and children. I'm sorry!"

Eddie pulled him back and pointed at him and Billy. "You will have the money here at this time tomorrow," Eddie said. "I know where you live. You don't want to see me again, understand?" They both nodded. "Now GET OUT!" Billy and Richie grabbed their coats and crept from the room.

I looked over at Stewie, who appeared to be in shock, and slowly let out my breath. Eddie turned to us, grinning. "Well, you guys, how'd I do?" he asked. Then his smile faded, replaced by a frown of concern. "You didn't think I was really going to throw that fat guy out the window, did you?"

"You could have fooled me," I said, shaking my head.

True to his word, Billy showed up the next day, right on time and with all our money. He apologized again and said it shouldn't have had to come down to that. We gazed at him silently. He shook his head, and left.

That was the end of our relationship with Lincoln Securities and Billy and Richie, and the beginning of the next chapter in our careers. In the fall of 1969, we went to work for Mark Serrano & Co. Within a year, Mark made Stewie and me partners.

Now we needed dealer's licenses. I'd heard the dealer exam was much harder than the trader's license test and I was terrified. After all, I was a P.E. teacher, not a stockbroker. I'd never had any economic or financial training. The test involved all kinds of economic principles I didn't know and required math expertise I didn't have. I didn't have a chance. But Mark told us not to worry. He knew a guy who guaranteed that anyone who took his four-day prep class would pass. He was expensive, but at this point, money wasn't an issue. We would have paid anything.

So we signed up and even paid extra for four days of private lessons. The results? We scored at the very top of the group, which included financial experts and college professors. Our ego trip took on legendary proportions. We were rich, market-savvy, and incredibly intelligent! (Interestingly, about a year later, the guy who trained us for the exam was busted for stock fraud.)

Now Mark was senior partner and owned 50 percent of the stock, and Stewie and I owned 25 percent each. Mark was in charge of the back office, the financial and accounting end of the business. Eventually Stewie headed up syndicate trading, and I was in charge of creating sales and motivating our brokers at the branch offices we opened around the country.

We continued with the same practices we had learned at North American Planning Corp., manipulating the market and making money hand over fist. Mark was as close to a rational being as we had at the company. At times he tried to bring some decorum and logic to the mix. Concerning the way we were moving as a company, he pleaded with us to be more long-range in our thinking, especially with respect to the huge amounts of money we were taking out of the business each week. Overall, we netted about $750,000 each month, not counting the inside stock we had from every underwriting. Mark, very sensibly, wanted to leave more money in the business to provide a solid foundation to operate from as we grew; he also wanted to diversify our financial base by finding other investment opportunities.

Stewie and I would have no part of it, especially Stewie. He got crazy anytime someone made a suggestion that would have compromised his huge paycheck. When it came time to cut checks, the three of us got into arguments every week, almost to the point of rage. Mark argued in favor of being more conservative, and Stewie and I would yell: "Just give us what we have coming to us! It's ours, we earned it, we don't want to hear about anything else!"

While it was true that we had earned our money, it was also true that we needed a certain amount for operating expenses. Mark and the accountants knew what those numbers were. The Federal Securities Exchange Commission, or SEC, required us to keep a minimum on hand to run the business, a sum that Mark and the accountants stuck to unequivocally. If it had been up to Stewie and me, we would have taken everything that wasn't nailed down.

In the end, however, even Mark got caught up in it all and simply wrote out the checks. After the screaming was over every week, the three of us would look at each other and break out laughing like crazed animals. We were three kids in a candy store.

Eventually, our accountants pointed out that if we continued to take extraordinary amounts of income each week, we would end up returning a huge chunk of it to the government at year's end. We'd been writing off expenses wherever possible to reduce our taxable income, but by then we'd run out of write-offs. Stewie and I were so drunk and dependent on our big weekly checks, we would have done anything to keep it going. In the back of our minds we always thought this whole game was too good to be true. We rationalized that if it all ended tomorrow, we had to take whatever we could now.

So one day we sat down with our accountants and asked what they thought we could do. They suggested we institute "nominee accounts" that involved putting family and friends on the payroll. We would issue payroll checks to them that they would return to us. In exchange, our accountants would do their taxes for free and the company would pay whatever income tax this extra "income" incurred. Our friends and family were happy to do it, because we would compensate them with new-issue stock when it opened. This was essentially a money laundering operation.

The accountants explained that the IRS would not consider it tax evasion if we actually paid taxes, and that nominee accounts were legal – admittedly a gray area, but as long as the taxes were paid, they assured us, we would be all right. It sounded wonderful, and also a bit wrong on some level. But we trusted our accountants – especially because they were showing us how to take home even more money. We signed up everyone we knew and ended up with about twenty nominees each.

It was this scheme that ultimately led to our demise. The nominee accounts were legal, but what allowed the State of New York to nail us was the fact that our books showed that people were earning money they didn't actually earn, which meant we were in violation of laws that prohibited "Falsifying the Books and Records of the Firm."

Not everyone was blasé about these legalities. People asked questions all the time, and that's where my talents came in, which I honed to a fine point. It was my job to keep everyone satisfied and "fired up." I became a master motivator, and quickly learned how to answer tricky questions and maneuver doubts into excitement. We didn't get much opposition from the trading department. Since we took good care of them financially, they had little to lose by following orders. One of the traders, Tim, who had been with Mark right from the beginning, was a straight-arrow kind of guy and liked to do everything by the book. In the end, if he wouldn't go along with us, we would get

Mark to speak to him. If Mark said it was okay, he went along, and of course Stewie and I kept the pressure on Mark all the time.

As the number of clients increased, we sought buying power in other directions. We hired more brokers and created branch offices, starting in New York. One of our top-producing brokers was Gene, a friend of Stewie's brother-in-law, whom we sent to Miami to open an office. Gene was a true politician who had a way of organizing things so that you assumed you were in charge, but actually he was in control. He was as smooth as they came – smooth as a shark. I never liked or trusted him, but because he made us a lot of money, I went along with most of his schemes.

Meanwhile, my old friend Marty, now in Los Angeles, was discovering that playing basketball, lying on the beach, and drinking Orange Juliuses was not paying the rent. He'd gotten his brokerage license and had started working in the stock market at about the time Stewie and I were looking to open an office on the West Coast. We made him manager of our new Los Angeles branch, which proved to be the perfect move. Marty had a way with people; besides, he was married to a hot young television writer named Sharon who connected him to wealthy, influential celebrities. By 1971, in addition to our three New York offices (one in the Bronx, affectionately known as "The Bronx Zoo," and two in Manhattan's financial district), and the ones in Miami and Los Angeles, we opened offices in Boston. We trained hundreds of new brokers and positioned them all over the country. Because of the company's rapid growth, it earned a reputation as the most exciting new investment firm on Wall Street.

The money poured in and we went crazy with it. We bought everything in sight: cars, clothes, houses. We ate at the most expensive restaurants. In fact, if the prices on the menu weren't exorbitant, we didn't bother with it. And we took outrageous vacations.

One day after a basketball game, Mark, Stewie, and I walked into a Cadillac dealership on a lark. We had come straight from the court, sweaty and disheveled in shorts and sneakers. We were ignored for some time until a salesman finally wandered over and blandly asked if he could help us.

I said, "We'll take four 'El D's,' with every option Cadillac offers. Two reds and two blues."

The salesman, about to faint, gathered his wits and asked how we wished to finance them. We smiled. "We'll pay cash," said Mark. The salesman gave us a price, Mark wrote out a check, and we left, the salesman staring at us with a look of astonishment.

At the time, an average car cost about $3,000. A fully-loaded El Dorado ran around $7,000. Mark took two: one for himself and one for his wife. I claimed a blue car, and Stewie a red one. Then I bought Ramona a station wagon, and Stewie bought his wife a Mercedes. I hadn't been much into clothes, and now everyone got after me to dress more sharply. I found a little French boutique in midtown called The Morning After and fell in love with the provocatively tight fit of their clothes. Everything I tried on looked amazing, even to me. A good suit in those days cost about $60; at this boutique, it cost $700.

And the food! We loved French, Italian and Castilian Spanish restaurants. At that time, an average bill in a nice restaurant might be $20 or $30 for two. We went to places that cost five to ten times that. One night at a fancy French restaurant, our dinner bill totaled $250. Even by today's standards a $250 meal is pricey, but in 1969, it was unbelievable. My rent was $69 a month. I was paying three-and-a-half times my rent for a single dinner! After we left the place that night, I complained to Ramona for hours about how outrageous the price was. But it was just for show. I reveled in the idea that I could afford such a place. I was glowing with pride for having that kind of money to spend on a single meal.

The vacations we took were just as lavish. Once, we flew first class to Hawaii and rented a fully equipped villa on the beach in Maui. The front door opened onto the sand and the back door opened onto an eighteen-hole professional golf course. Our week's stay cost almost $10,000 – about twice what I had made the year before as a teacher.

Chapter 7:

Greed

Around the end of 1969, Ramona and I moved into a magnificent three-bedroom penthouse apartment in Riverdale, an exclusive suburb at the northernmost point of Manhattan. We had spectacular 360-degree views of the New York skyline to the south, the Palisades and Hudson River to the west, the Catskill mountains to the north and the Whitestone and Throggs Neck bridges to the east. My next-door neighbor was Willie Mays, who was just finishing his career with the New York Mets.

Ramona hired an interior decorator. We covered the 2,600 square-foot terrace, which wrapped around the apartment, with Astroturf, the new artificial surface being used on professional football and baseball fields. We spent a small fortune creating a terrace garden with custom-made redwood planters and flowering plants, trees and shrubs. We had to hire a gardener to take care of it all.

In less than a month, Ramona managed to spend well over $100,000 on furniture, most of which she purchased from designer stores that were so exclusive you had to know someone to get in. The interior decorator's commission was close to $20,000. Ramona bought plush white carpeting to cover the foyer, dining room, and living room. Visitors were almost intimidated by the opulence of it all. For our housewarming party, we invited almost a hundred guests and hired the great Ray Barretto and his salsa orchestra. I grumbled to Ramona every step of the way, but she kept saying, "Stop complaining! You love it." And she was right. What I loved (besides the charge I got out of knowing I could afford it) was that the apartment was comfortable and welcoming. We could hardly believe it — me, a middle-class Jewish kid from the Bronx and Ramona, an innocent Latin girl from the South Bronx, living in splendor.

But little by little, and imperceptibly to myself, I was becoming arrogant, selfish, and insensitive. Busy savoring all the attention I was getting, I didn't notice how I was treating others. Now that I had money, I wanted people to recognize my accomplishments. I wanted them to need me and I wanted to rub my success in their faces. In my fantasies, I was a benevolent king. My humble former associates would beg for my audience, grovel at my feet, and I would compassionately "see how I might help them" when I had a moment to spare. I longed to get back at everyone I thought had wronged me. I wanted to stand separate from and above the masses who might wish to get close to me.

My brother Lou, seven and a half years older than me, came

to visit me in the office one day. He'd always been the family success and was very business-wise. I had always been jealous of his success and self-confidence, as well as intimidated and envious of him. I coveted the respect he got. I thought him insensitive, egotistical, and aloof. It never occurred to me that I was describing myself.

All my life I had gone to him. Now, at last, he had come to me. When he walked into my office, my secretary buzzed me on the intercom. She said my brother was out front, waiting to see me. I felt my face flush and my heart pound. At the thought of him sitting out there waiting for me, the unexpressed bitterness, anger, jealousy, and blame I had hoarded for so long rose up like bile.

I left him sitting out in the front office for almost two hours. He finally stormed out. He didn't speak to me for two months. When I came to my senses, I called to apologize. I made up some story about what a hectic day it had been, so hectic that I hadn't heard my secretary when she announced him. It was mostly a lie, of course. Although I hadn't intended for him to sit out there for as long as he did, I'd relished the notion that my big, successful brother was, for once, waiting for me. And when I got so caught up in my head, I actually did forget him. As resentful and angry as I was toward him, I did admire and love him. Yet I allowed myself to forget all about him, to humiliate and frustrate him – my big brother who had come just to tell me how proud he was of me.

From time to time it occurred to me that there had to be

a catch to this runaway success, but the excitement and thrill of it never let me seriously consider that there was something wrong with what we were doing. No one else did, either. They all had the same disease Stewie and I had – Greed – and the same psychological and emotional handicaps as well. At a deep level, everyone knew what was going on, but no one wanted the game to end. No one wanted to think that he was doing something wrong. The game was just too sweet, too exciting to think of stopping.

Every day was pandemonium. Stocks continued to run wild, huge trades brought in enormous amounts of money, new issues were always about to open. This was the early 70's, and our brokers were making $150,000 to $300,000 a year – the equivalent of millions in today's dollars. It was unthinkable to do anything that would interrupt the flow of fancy cars, huge homes, expensive jewelry, beautiful women, and an abundance of recognition, attention and power. So we all played the game together. Everyone's making money, right? The company, the brokers, the customers – all of us were raking it in. What could be wrong with making money? We were doing a good thing. These were the daily conversations we had alone and amongst ourselves, until after a while, we all believed it.

Three years passed. By 1972 the business had grown to staggering levels of prosperity. We had over 200 employees in six offices in four cities. The company grossed $10 million to $12 million a year. As our buying power increased, our success created such attention throughout the financial community that thirty-five of the most prominent over-the-counter brokerage houses sought us out to form an underwriting syndicate.

An underwriting syndicate is a group of investment banking firms or brokerage houses that get together on a public offering, to share in the selling of the securities. This usually occurs when the amounts of money to be raised are too large for any one company to handle by itself. Our syndicate was looser in its workings than what you'd normally see. Besides the usual functions of a syndicate, we were also interested in using each other to warehouse stocks, to move customers around and create paper profits. For example, if a customer was in a stock for a year, we would pull him out and move him into a different stock, one that one of our syndicate firms was trading. In return, we bought one of the syndicate firm's stocks and put the customer we had just sold into that. This generated commissions both to the house and to the individual brokers, along with a show of movement and profit for the customer. The lead underwriter earned compensation as well, getting a percentage that depended on how much stock a syndicate member purchased from us.

As time went by, we developed new relationships with other investment banking houses and brokerage firms similar to us in size and activity with new issues, trading stocks from inventory, and so on. As we became well known and our stocks became the talk of The Street, we ended up with 35 brokerage houses in our syndicate. We were now making more money every day than anyone ever could have imagined – enough to stop working and live like kings for the rest of our lives. Stewie and I even talked about buying our own private islands to live on. But underneath all the fantasies and the delusions of power, I began to sense that something bad was about to happen.

I was so involved with the business that I was getting run down physically. I was eating and drinking too much, smoking more than ever. I'd even started smoking cigars. I rarely found time to work out, something that had been an essential part of my life. I was burning out, and no longer felt good physically or emotionally. I knew it would take more than a vacation to get me re-ignited.

When I mentioned this to Stewie he thought I was crazy. In his mind, there was no stopping. We were about to reach a whole new level, and he was more excited than ever. In vain I tried to convince him that it was time to think about getting out and moving on. And as the business grew, so did my family. Ramona gave birth to Alana, our first child, in February 1971. Over the next few years, Adam and Jason were born. Now I really had it all: money, success, love, power and family.

My outer circumstances couldn't possibly have been better. I had more money and success than I knew what to do with and was surrounded by people who constantly told me how great I was. But I had completely lost myself in it all and was beginning to realize just how lost I was. Mentally exhausted and emotionally drained, my dreams at night were heavy, negative and frightening.

One morning I woke up stunned with the worst sense of fear I'd ever had in my life. That morning, I woke with the feeling I had come out of a profound darkness where there was no joy and no light. The fear began even before I opened my eyes. A knot had formed in the pit of my stomach, a sense of being all alone in the world, although Ramona was asleep right next to me.

Usually I could find something to ground me. I'd snuggle up to Ramona and feel temporarily secure and safe. Or I'd think positive thoughts about the new day, anticipating the pleasure of going to the office and hanging out with the brokers under me who had become friends. Or I would pick up the phone and call Stewie, who could always make me laugh. One by one, however, these antidotes to fear no longer soothed me. Hanging out with Stewie, having sex, working out, drinking, smoking pot and cigarettes – every one of them had failed me over the past months, and this morning I knew I was absolutely alone with my fear and depression.

What was going on? I could understand depression arising from a lack of success or love, or from tragedy. But my life seemed perfect, except for the fact that I was still haunted by the face of the sad little boy in that old photograph. And because everything I had done since the day I found it was an attempt to change my state, it showed me so clearly just how far from perfect my life really was.

I had raced after whatever I thought could change my feelings and give me a better handle on life. Sports, girls, school, music, sex all seemed promising at first and gave me hope, but each eventually left me empty and more depressed than before. The final promise for true happiness was money and all that went with it. Everything else had failed me. This had to be it. But now that I had filled my pockets with gold, I was more depressed, lonely, and scared than ever before. At that moment I realized I had run out of options. The walls of my life were closing in. There was nowhere else to go. For a moment, I even contemplated suicide, to get rid of that fear and loneliness. But I was too afraid to die. Finally, I did the one thing I knew how to do: I got up and went to work. I shifted my focus, shoved down the fear, and dove back into my business.

Unfortunately, the panic attack that morning was just another in a series of wake-up calls I chose to ignore.

Chapter 8:

Payback

A few days later, in early 1972, I received a literal wake-up call. The jangle of the bedside phone dragged me from yet another heavy sleep. It was Stewie, who asked, "Have you heard the news?"

"What news?" I responded groggily.

"The NASD has suspended us from trading," he said. He was referring to the National Association of Securities Dealers. "They've padlocked our door and we're under investigation for stock fraud. I just got a call from Mark. There's an emergency meeting at the office for the entire company. We need to be there immediately!"

About twenty people were crowded into my office, leaving barely enough room for me and Stewie to wriggle in. Mark was sitting coolly behind my desk. All talk stopped as we entered.

These were our brokers. Every one of them had invested in our stocks. They all bought stock in our new issues illegally, under assumed names, and they were all scared and angry because every one of them stood to lose all of their money. Mark gestured for us to sit down. He explained that the NASD had temporarily suspended the company from trading for violating the net capital rule – we'd allowed our liquid net capital to fall below the required minimum. Such a penalty can be disastrous for a company because people checking the value of their stocks will see, rather than price quotes, the words: SUSPENDED FROM TRADING. Stock owners panic. As soon as the suspension is lifted, a sell-off begins, which causes stock prices to drop drastically. In our case, this would devalue not only our inventory but the inventories of our syndicate, putting each company in violation of the net capital rule. Unless we did something immediately, Mark said, the company faced bankruptcy.

"I don't want to see anybody get hurt," he said, "but if the company goes bankrupt, thousands of investors will be ruined, along with all of us. Since I own 50 percent of the stock, I'll put $100,000 of my personal funds into the company – *if* Stewie and Alan contribute $50,000 each."

Silence. Stewie and I looked at each other, reluctant to give up any of our wealth. Before we had a chance to respond, though, there was a commotion at the front of the room. Jim Gordon was standing, and he was yelling. Worse, he was waving a gun.

"You guys are responsible for everything that's happened!" he shouted. "You never cared about anything but filling your own pockets. All of us here are on the verge of losing everything we ever had in our lives." He pointed the gun at Stewie and me. "And it's all your fault! I want to hear you say, in this room, that you will put the money up to save this company. And God help you if you don't!"

Jim was a broker, a tough Irishman, and an old friend of Mark's who had worked as a bouncer in bars and clubs around the city for most of his life. Everyone liked him, including me. But that afternoon it was a different ballgame. The look in his eyes left no doubt that he was capable of taking this threat all the way. Stewie and I nearly wet our pants. We assured him we would put in the money. Jim holstered his gun, and everyone applauded.

The money we put in did give us some operating capital. The suspension was lifted and we began trading again, so we were still technically in business. But it was too little, too late. The minute we re-opened our doors, our customers began selling off their stock, and it never stopped.

Much later, we were outraged to learn from the IRS (which, along with the SEC and the Securities Investors Protection Insurance Corp., was investigating us) that Mark never did put in his share. We wanted our money back but knew Mark would never willingly hand it over. Stewie and I agreed that the scam we'd pulled on Billy and Richie of Lincoln Securities – intimidating them with a couple of scary-looking thugs – had worked quite nicely, and we might as well try it on Mark.

We hired two mob hit men, members of one of the biggest organized-crime families in New York, who were moonlighting as bodyguards. They looked nothing like we would have expected. One was balding, the other wore glasses. Other than that, they were almost identical – middle-aged, flea-bitten guys who looked dumpy, dirty, and tired. We explained the situation and told them not to load their guns.

"Don't worry," they said. "We know what to do. We'll just scare him good. We'll get your money for you."

Stewie and I and our hired guns met Mark at a restaurant in Manhattan. Stewie had set up the meeting by telling Mark that we'd come up with a great idea that could get us all out of this mess. When Mark arrived, he looked cool and relaxed. But the minute he sat down, we went right at him. We pointed out that he'd ripped us off and was responsible for us losing our money. We said he owed us a hundred grand and we intended to get it.

He hardly blinked. "You take your two goons and do whatever you gotta do, but you're getting nothing from me," he said.

One of our thugs went for the gun that was stuck in his waistband. Somehow he lost his grip and it fell down his pants leg. He sat there, groping in his pants, embarrassed.

Mark just laughed. "You know what else?" he said. "That whole scene with Jim Gordon and the gun? All faked. Just like the one I helped you pull on those jerks from Lincoln Securities. Payback's a bitch, ain't it?"

Then he stood up, looked us squarely in the eye, and walked out.

Stewie and I lost millions of dollars in inventory and stock. Thousands of our investors, including family and friends, lost their entire life savings. Prominent businessmen, world-famous athletes, and celebrities all went down the same way. We began receiving hate calls and death threats.

My own father, who went to work for me after he retired, had invested most of his money in the stocks I recommended. He lost every cent. He was doubly devastated because not only was all his retirement money gone, but his son – whom he'd become very close to and depended on so much – was facing grand larceny charges, public disgrace, lawsuits, and a long prison sentence.

Because Mark Serrano & Co. had the most buying power of the houses in our syndicate, we were able to stay solvent while everyone else went bankrupt. We tried to save as many of the others as possible by buying back huge blocks of stock from their inventories. But one by one, day after day, they toppled. Within six months every member of the syndicate, except for us, was brought to its knees.

Stewie and I, however, were the main focus of the investigation. The District Attorney had no intention of prosecuting everyone; there were too many people involved. For reasons of expediency, the attorney general decided only to go after the guys at the top. To the three hundred or so brokers in our branch offices across the country – all of whom were doing, on a smaller scale, the same things we were – the DA offered immunity in exchange for information.

Gene, the broker from our Miami office, was instrumental in organizing the other brokers and getting them to accept the immunity deal. Family members and lifelong friends, whom I loved and trusted, accepted the same deal and became informants, giving the DA everything he asked for. How could people that close to me turn against me so readily? Their depositions became the foundation for the criminal indictments that followed. The first indictments were handed down in late spring of 1972. Stewie and I were charged by the state of New York with 79 counts of grand larceny and stock fraud. Even though Mark owned 50 percent of the company, and the company and all the stock was in his name, he was able to convince the authorities and our employees that Stewie and Alan were the culprits. Two years later, the U.S. Attorney's Office, representing the SEC, indicted us again. This time they indicted Mark as well.

But I was beginning to wake up to my responsibility for what was happening. I was still angry, but beginning to look at the truth. I knew that people really weren't being unfair by testifying against me. I was not *actually* being betrayed. The crisis was making me look at myself. It was *my* actions, and mine alone, that had brought me to this. Much later, I would come to understand that although the whole world seemed to be against me, and the pain and fear were intense, this drama actually put me on the path to discovering my true self and would begin to set me free.

Chapter 9:

The "Sit-Down"

Sharks are drawn to carnage. A bit of blood in the water, and a shark-fest ensues. One day shortly after we were suspended from trading, I got a call from a high profile, notorious, underworld figure named Jerry Fine.

Jerry was a front man for the mob and was known all over New York City as "The King of Pornography." He controlled the smut parlors, peep shows, and X-rated bookstores around Times Square. Recently he'd been the front-page focus of an exposé on porn in the city, about which a criminal investigation had been going on for weeks.

He came right to the point over the phone: He had half a million dollars invested with us, and he wanted it back. Since his loss was a direct result of our illegal activities, we were accountable. Stewie and I arranged to meet him at our office, hoping we could persuade him to back off.

I was surprised when I saw him: He didn't look like a gangster. Here was a living version of the cartoon character Yosemite Sam – short and squat, with red hair and a beard, and far from friendly. But he was too menacing to be comical. We explained we'd all lost a lot of money, even our immediate families and closest friends. We pointed out that the account in question was in his father's name. His father had handled all the transactions; we never had dealt with anyone else.

Jerry waved us off. He didn't care who else had lost money. He didn't care whose name was on the account. It was his money, and he was there to claim it. Then he paused, stared coldly at us, and snarled, "The next time I see you, you will have my money." And he stalked out the door.

Stewie and I looked at each other. What had we gotten into now? It was bad enough that we'd lost millions and had legions of angry people threatening us. But going up against the Mafia was a whole different trip.

Scared and confused, we ran to a lawyer recommended by a principal at one of our syndicate member companies. He listened to our story. "This is beyond anything that can be resolved by the police," he said. "We need to arrange a 'sit-down.' Leave it to me. I know some people who are connected. I'll set up a meeting. We'll get you a couple of bodyguards from a different family than Jerry's. They'll protect you and represent you at the sit-down, so you'll get a fair shot." (As it turned out, he was scheming to grab a huge cut from what we would pay our bodyguards.)

Within a few days Stewie and I met at the lawyer's office and were introduced to our protectors. We settled the question of payment and told our story. The bodyguards said they knew Jerry's "people" and were willing to arrange a sit-down. One of them peered over his glasses at us and issued a warning. "You are answerable for half a million dollars," he said, jabbing a finger for emphasis. "If the decision goes against you, you'll have to come up with the money. There is no appeal." Most of my assets were gone, along with my once mighty cash reserves. I had no idea what I would do if the decision went against us, but I had no other options.

Several days later, I met Stewie and our bodyguards on Sixth Avenue and Forty-second Street. Stewie's tailored suit made him look much too affluent, I thought. On closer inspection, I realized his face was a sickly green. If I hadn't been so scared myself, I would have burst out laughing. I probably looked as bad as he did. I hadn't eaten or slept in days.

As we walked the few blocks to our rendezvous, our representatives explained the rules of the proceedings: Jerry's family would run the trial and make the final decision. I glanced over at Stewie, whose complexion had gone from sickly green to deathly white. I felt like I was trudging to my execution.

We entered a rundown, nondescript office building and climbed a rickety flight of stairs. Two thugs at the top, who looked like retired NFL linemen, ushered us into a spartan room that had been recently painted. There was a long conference table. The door shut behind us and the thugs took their positions blocking the exit.

A dozen or so people from Jerry's family were in the room. Facing us across the table was a distinguished-looking man whose air of authority left no doubt about who was in charge. His hair was slicked back; he looked like the former New York Knicks coach, Pat Riley. In his expensive suit, he was the perfect GQ Mafia stereotype – manicured, tailored, smooth, detached. He was the judge. Without ever speaking, he gestured, and people moved.

Someone motioned us into seats opposite him. Jerry rose and presented his case. Any likeness to the cartoon character evaporated. He presented himself as the innocent victim of a plot to swindle him out of his money. Stewie and I, he said, were common criminals who had ruthlessly taken advantage of Jerry's father, an unsuspecting old man. We were outrageous. We were immoral. He began repeating himself, getting worked up, and so angry that everyone in the room, especially the "Don" running the sit-down, started to fidget.

I didn't understand why Jerry was taking such an aggressive stance. All he had to do was state the facts; these guys didn't care about morals. They knew the outcome before they arrived; family stuck together. They just wanted to get this thing over with and leave. But Jerry went on and on. When he finally finished, it was my turn.

I stood. I knew that Jerry had dramatically distorted what had happened. I sensed that everybody else knew it too and disliked him for it. His anger tipped the balance of power and gave me a chance. My fear evaporated. I became centered, focused, and infused with energy, power and confidence. I stopped thinking about who was in the room or what might happen to me. I was in The Zone. The words came as effortlessly as when I was playing basketball and the shots went in when I forgot myself. When I was finished, the room reverberated with energy. I was exhilarated.

Stewie and I were escorted into the hallway to await the decision. He whispered, "Where did *that* come from?"

Physically and emotionally drained, I smiled and shrugged. Whatever the outcome, I was all right either way.

After a short wait, one of the guards opened the door and poked his head out. "The ruling went in your favor," he said. "It's over! Go home!"

In January 1974, just before we were scheduled to go to trial, Stewie and I accepted a plea bargain offered by the New York attorney general. We pleaded guilty to one count of falsifying the books and records of the firm in exchange for two years of probation and six months of community service.

The day we went to court for sentencing, the room was packed with family and friends. The sentencing judge was outraged by the extent of the financial damage we had wrought. He totally rejected our attorney's plea for leniency, citing the fact that we had hurt so many people. His final intention was to send us to jail.

We were then asked if we had anything to tell the judge in our own defense. The moment we began speaking we completely fell apart. We stood in front of the judge begging for mercy. "We're not really brokers, we're just schoolteachers," we said. "We didn't know what we were doing. We have kids. Our families depend on us. We'll do anything you ask, but please don't send us to prison!" For a moment Stewie and I really did fear we were going to jail and we wept openly at the thought. Our wives and children cried. Our brothers, sisters, in-laws, and friends cried. Everyone seemed genuinely touched, even the people that were so angry at us for defrauding them. The only dry eyes in the courtroom belonged to the judge. Finally, he looked at the prosecutor and said, "I can't do it!" We received five years of probation and a year of community service. And of course, we were barred from ever working in the financial industry again.

Outside the courtroom, the tears we wiped away were tears of laughter. "We did it again!" I said, trying to hide my giggles from the probation officer. "We closed the judge!" Through all this, we hadn't learned anything. I was so relieved that I didn't want to think about it, and making light of it distracted me from realizing how much pain I had caused. Part of me knew exactly what I was doing: It was the old manipulative tendency working at its best. Only this time, instead of bringing me more money, I was using my skills to avoid a prison sentence.

Next the federal government indicted us for securities fraud. It took until 1977 to arrange a plea bargain on those charges, and we were required to make restitution. The feds really wanted

Mark Serrano, who had escaped prosecution by the State. Mark had persuaded everyone that the firm's demise and its fraudulent practices were the work of Stewie and me. But the SEC was much more sophisticated than the state attorney general's office. Their investigators knew that a couple of gym teachers with no prior business experience could not possibly have masterminded the escapade alone. They knew Mark was a big part of it and wanted to nail him, but they had no corroborating testimony. They told us that if we answered their questions they'd recommend we get no jail time and the case would end. We had no problem with that.

Chapter 10:

Independence

Long before our legal problems were resolved, Stewie and I were faced with a more immediate problem: how to make a living. It was 1973, we were in the middle of the indictments for securities charges, and my life was in shreds. I was 34 and unemployed. Most of my money was gone, and I couldn't return to the investment business. At the same time, I didn't want to give up my lavish lifestyle, and I clung to the illusion of self-worth that money still gave me.

Stewie and I began planning our next move. We wanted to make it big again. We were cocky even now, despite our losses. If we made it big once, we could do it again. After all, we were still young, driven and in possession of unparalleled sales talent. While some of this was bravado, part was true. We leaned on each other, pumping each other up, maintaining the belief that we could do anything we put our minds to. I searched *The New York Times* for sales jobs. Besides the stock market, what industry would give us the best shot for the big bucks? The obvious answer was real estate.

A *Times* ad for people to sell land and homes in Pennsylvania's Pocono Mountains claimed that top salesmen could earn $5,000 a week. Stewie and I figured this could be an ideal opportunity to make a killing. We went for an interview and met with one of the managers who explained that the job involved bringing families from metropolitan New York to a four-season recreational community in the Poconos. Since the development was under construction while the property was being sold, potential investors had a chance to purchase land at a price far below that of developed property. The manager made it sound both legitimate and easy, and Stewie and I bought right into it.

Quickly we discovered that the business was far from legitimate; it was the same old mix of greed, deceit and false dealings. But we were both very, very good at it, and in the end our customers owned an actual piece of property rather than some worthless pieces of paper. Bolstered by the possibility of making big money again, Stewie and I worked night and day. Within a few months I became the top producer in the company, with Stewie not far behind. No one could figure out how we were doing it.

The secret was our relationship. Stewie and I were partners. We had always worked as a team and split everything fifty-fifty. We trusted each other implicitly, something others found hard to understand. And we always covered for each other, which gave us leverage. If I needed a potential buyer taken care of,

Stewie would do it, and vice-versa. We both loved being in the spotlight. My ego was once again receiving all the accolades it could handle. All this attention worked like a drug: It got me high and drove me to work harder and produce more. I couldn't get enough.

One afternoon after a sales meeting, the president of the land development company called me to his office. I was flattered but a bit uneasy, because most salesmen never got to see him privately. But he was friendly, and thanked me for all the business I'd brought in. He said that in all these years he had never seen anyone sell with as much enthusiasm and energy. Then he offered me a managerial position with an opportunity to earn even more.

Then it struck me that he hadn't mentioned Stewie. "Stewie and I are partners," I said. "Can I assume that Stewie is part of the deal?"

"The offer is for you alone," he said. "Stewie's a good salesman, but it's you I want as my manager."

I wanted this opportunity, but I worried it would wreck my relationship with Stewie. I went to Stewie and unfolded my conversation with the president. Though he made light of it and said it was okay with him if I accepted the offer, I could see that it hurt him.

In the end, I just couldn't do it. We'd come too far together; I owed him more than that. I also felt I needed him. I had become dependent on the confidence and security I got from him. But that dependency also made me feel trapped. It would have been easy merely to avoid the issue and move on as I always had, but this time something wouldn't let me. I was being asked to look at this matter directly, painful as it was. I knew that as long as I needed Stewie or anyone else for support, I'd always feel trapped, and I'd always be afraid. I yearned to break loose, to let go, to be free, but I wasn't ready to do it.

Shortly afterward, I got a call from a former company salesman named Lloyd, who left because he'd been offered a better opportunity. He was making big money as general manager of a new development and was looking for a dynamic guy with the ability to significantly boost sales. He said I was the best land salesman he'd ever seen, and he would feel confident with me in charge of marketing. I could hire my own staff. I'd be responsible for all the costs and expenses of running my end of the business, but I'd be given 40 percent of the weekly gross for the entire development. Most of the strong land developments at that time were producing between half a million and a million dollars a week. So at 40 percent, after things got going, we would probably gross at least a half a million a week! My heart began to pound.

As I told Stewie about Lloyd and his proposition, he became excited again for the first time in weeks. This new opportunity was our chance to bond again as partners and friends. In spite of my recent insight about my dependence on Stewie, I wasn't ready to go it alone. I was still attached, still saying it would be easier to have Stewie around shouldering some of the load.

It took a month to work out all the details. In the end, we faced only one obstacle: the company's racial policy. At the time, most developments shared the tacit understanding that salesmen did not solicit blacks. This made me extremely uncomfortable. Up until then I had gone along with this policy because of the money. But now, my love for my wife and my concern for her feelings had become more important to me. The awareness that I really loved Ramona grew. And this awareness compelled me to trust what I felt was right.

As a result, I no longer felt comfortable operating under the policy about not selling to minorities, and was ready to walk away from the whole scene unless things changed radically. When Lloyd saw how strongly I felt about the issue, he softened his position, although he insisted we keep the numbers of minority families to a "reasonable" level. That wasn't good enough. After much intense discussion, Lloyd finally agreed to open the community to everyone. I was ecstatic, and Ramona seemed relieved. It had never occurred to me that she, a woman of color, was affronted when she entered the development. Although she had always kept her uneasiness to herself, she now opened up to me about how terribly unwelcome she'd felt. She even saw this as an opportunity to get her real estate license and become a salesperson. Ramona was talented and enthusiastic and I knew she'd be a natural. I loved that idea. We could be together more, especially on the long weekend drives to Pennsylvania.

Within a few months, we were selling close to forty lots a week – almost $300,000 in volume – and sales continued to soar. Stewie and I were about to make more money than ever before, even at the crest of our stock-market days. We now employed about twenty-five salesmen, half of them black or Hispanic. We had tapped into a wide-open market previously untargeted because of bigotry. Now the possibilities were unlimited. The money was great, and I felt good about what I was doing. I loved to see people so happy as they left the property with their deeds. For so many, owning their own home on a good piece of land was a lifelong dream. I was helping to make that dream a reality, and that fulfilled me – but not for long.

Stewie, his wife Lila, Ramona and I stayed at a Holiday Inn each weekend while working at the property. One evening in the fall of 1974 Stewie and Lila came to our room. Stewie had something hard and unpleasant to say. Finally, he got it out. The owner had issued an ultimatum: Stop bringing black and minority families to the property.

I felt sick.

Apparently, property owners already living in the development had begun organizing protest groups, petitioning the company heads to do something about "all the black people running around on our property." They threatened legal action, and violence had already broken out. Salesmen's cars had been broken into, tires slashed and windows broken. Someone had blown out all four tires of a property director's Jeep with a shotgun.

Angry groups had stormed the sales office, cursing and shouting at potential buyers, especially if they were black. They wanted no black or Hispanic sales people on the property either, including Ramona. The owner told Stewie that if we failed to desist bringing "those people" to the property, he would close down the operation.

As Stewie spoke, tears welled up in his eyes. Ramona sat motionless. I felt angry and violated; I knew what was coming. Stewie said he understood how I felt about "this whole racial thing," but he was convinced that there was nothing we could do about it.

"We're on the brink of making another fortune, Alan!" he said. "In another year or two we can both walk away, set for the rest of our lives."

All the years that Stewie and I had worked together came down to this moment. Our friendship and our partnership were on the line. I could choose Stewie, and the security of a fortune, or I could choose my principles and walk away.

Ramona came over to where I sat and looked into my eyes. "I understand that this place is where we earn our money," she said softly. "If you decide to continue working here, I'll always stand behind you, but I can no longer be part of it. You do what you think best, but I'll never come back here again."

Ramona had also been growing as a person. I knew that if I stayed, she would honor her promise to support me, but our marriage would never be the same. I did not want to lose her. I was tempted to take the money and rationalize my hypocrisy to Ramona and myself. But something would not let me do that. Her decision helped me choose. Once again I felt this great energy inside that was more powerful than my greed or my fear. My choice became obvious. I chose my heart.

I turned to Stewie. "I'm leaving," I said. "I can't do this anymore, and not just for Ramona, but for myself too. I need to find something that is real, that has meaning. If I don't, I'll die inside. This is not who I am anymore."

As I spoke, I was filled with a profound sense of power and humility. For the first time in my life, I'd chosen to follow my heart rather than my need for material security. That choice gave me an experience of unbelievable strength and conviction, qualities that previously I had attributed to outer success.

Stewie gaped at me. "Are you crazy?" he cried. "Do you know how much money you're walking away from?"

I was trembling, but stood firm. "It's over, Stewie," I said. "I'm leaving." I turned to face Ramona, and let her pain wash over me. I held her, my heart bursting with love, while we both cried.

Much was on my mind as we drove back to New York the next day. I was nervous and apprehensive, but not because I was second-guessing my decision. I simply had no idea what I was going to do with the rest of my life. My dreams that night were polluted by uncertainties and doubts. Negative thoughts left me feeling heavy, as though I'd overeaten or drunk too much. This newly emerging consciousness in my life gave me the courage to end my relationship with Stewie, and, despite how frightening it was, to follow my intuition about what was right for me. Still, I wasn't ready to give up my extravagant lifestyle;

my consciousness hadn't reached that level yet. I was worried about my future. How would I manage?

The next morning, I awoke feeling rejuvenated, as if a great weight had been lifted. The weight, I knew, was the accumulation of all the wrong choices I'd made over the years. Choices made for money, recognition and respect. Choices of situations that would feed my ego. Choices of people who praised, flattered and mollified me. At last I could see my true motives: Making money for people gave me control over them. I was glad to remove myself from that scene. The voice of my heart had begun to rise above the chatter of my insecurities.

Chapter 11:

Kid Harlem

What lay in store? How would I make it from now on? I was on probation for securities violations; I had just quit the land business and ended my partnership with Stewie. The overhead I'd created for my family and myself was enormous. Our lifestyle would soon exhaust our savings. The year before we had purchased a 5,000-square-foot estate in the plush Westchester suburb of Chappaqua. (Yes, with the last of my money I bought a house while I was right in the middle of the investigation by the state of New York. Stewie had said, "Buy the house! We're going to be on top again.") We had a live-in housekeeper and a groundskeeper. We had lavish wardrobes and fancy cars. I had no income, but Ramona and I were determined to hold onto this way of life.

There was one easy solution: I could sell drugs.

For most of my life I'd avoided the drug scene. As an athlete,

I was careful about my physical condition, and the fear of getting hooked kept me straight. Gradually, though, I began to notice that drug use was becoming almost commonplace. Celebrities, professional athletes, and corporate executives were smoking pot and snorting cocaine. When I was about thirty, I began to experiment, first with marijuana, then, a few years later, cocaine. I indulged mostly at parties, or to enhance sex, or as a boost to my mood or my energy. The illusion that "everyone was doing it" enabled me to rationalize and justify my own use. And the more I rationalized, the more relaxed about it I became.

I had been buying pot and coke from a friend of Ramona's – a big-time drug dealer named Diego. Diego was married to Ramona's best friend, Aida. Ramona and Aida had known each other since they were little girls. We were friends, and trusted each other. Getting larger quantities from Diego was no problem. I found that I could cover the exorbitant costs by "cutting" the package (adding an artificial ingredient to double or triple the quantity), then sell it at a good price. I didn't regard myself as a drug dealer, but by 1975, that's exactly what I had become.

I was conservative about it all. I wasn't out there soliciting. I only dealt with friends and other trustworthy people. My goal was to make enough to support my lifestyle. I usually did a few transactions a week of $700 to $1,000 each, bringing in $2,000 to $3,000. It didn't compare to what I made before, but it was more than enough because there was no overhead (other than the cost of the drugs) and I certainly didn't pay income tax.

I started to accumulate some real money again, but obviously couldn't open a bank account with dirty money. So I rented a safety deposit box and gradually filled it with hundred-dollar bills. I felt like a kid playing Monopoly. I paid for everything I could in cash.

Selling drugs not only preserved my lifestyle, it also granted me a lot of free time. Before, I'd always structured my life around my business, my interests, whatever promoted my shallow desires. I used my family to feel secure and important. I never wanted to look at that, but I knew they felt it. Though I regarded my wife and children as the essence of my life, the truth was I was too insecure to open myself to them. Once in a while I was aware of how insensitive I'd become, and that brought up tremendous fear and shame. Sometimes I saw such sadness in their faces that it made me sick. I realized in those moments how much I'd hurt them, yet how much I loved them. I wanted to change this, and bring us closer together.

And so, with the gift of time that came with selling drugs, I could slow down and re-create our family. We began to live freely and spontaneously. I would load the kids into the car and take them everywhere – food shopping, movies, restaurants, the zoo. I became relaxed and happy, and free of the guilt of having excluded them in the past. I loved this freedom. I didn't have to go anywhere or do anything. As time went on, wanting solitude, I spent whole afternoons out on the lawn, just pulling weeds. I was able to relax completely. My mind would drift peacefully.

Sometimes, as I sat weeding the lawn, I'd look up at the sky, inhaling the fresh, sweet air. Bliss filled me. It seemed the world had stopped and I'd entered a magical timelessness. I'd never known such sweetness in the rushed, hyped-up life I had been leading. I knew that selling drugs was wrong but pushed the thought away. It was easier to bask in serenity. How could something as pure as this tranquility come from something that wasn't innocent?

Drug dealers must be careful about whom they deal with. They must surround themselves with people they can trust, especially when it comes to employees. I realized I needed to find someone to insulate me by doing the actual selling. The only person I could trust was my closest friend in the world, my soul buddy Joey.

I met Joey in 1973 in the Poconos, when I was selling land at the development. He was an amazing artist and craftsman who could create mind-blowing things out of his imagination: model boats, walking sticks, engravings and etchings of all kinds. The extraordinary thing about our relationship was that he never wanted anything from me – or from anyone else, for that matter. He was the most independent, free-spirited being I'd ever met. He was like an alley cat, a nomadic street person without a permanent home. He lived in the moment, moved with the wind, and did as he pleased. I came to love him, as did everyone who really got to know him.

As far as dealing drugs went, his free-spirited nature could create problems for me and for himself, but I was willing to take the risk. And so I discussed my idea with him, and he agreed immediately. Dealing turned out to be the perfect role for him because it allowed him to circulate freely. He had an uncanny ability to develop relationships with famous athletes and celebrities at hip parties and trendy bars. He was in his element. In those days it seemed as if everyone was using drugs, which translated into an automatic market for me. I had the connections. Joey cultivated the relationships, set up the sales, delivered the drugs, and collected the money. He saw it all as a game.

It occurred to me that my neighbors might wonder why I never went to work. Although we kept a low profile, I felt I should do something to prevent raised eyebrows. I'd already accumulated enough cash to open some legitimate business, one that would be fun and profitable. The drug dealing had to end. It had served its purpose, had given me the time I needed to get my head together and make some money. I never meant for it to last forever.

I needed a "front" to justify where and how I lived. With nothing particular in mind, I began to search for the right situation. As soon as I made an intention to go for it, everything fell into place. One day a young friend of mine, Richie, came to my house. I hadn't seen him in a while. Richie had run a "boiler room" operation for me when I was in real estate sales, cranking out hundreds of cold calls daily. He was the godfather of our youngest child, Jason, and I regarded him as another son.

As an all-star athlete in high school and college, he'd attracted the interest of both the NFL and professional baseball teams, until he busted up his knee during a college football game.

Although only in his early twenties, Richie always handled everything with mature ease. His telemarketing crew functioned twelve hours a day, with over sixty phones going in three shifts, and accounted for a half million dollars a week in business. He was bright, handsome, and charismatic, with enough personality and talent to become a movie star if he'd wanted to. Women fell all over him. He got everything he wanted, and it could have been easy to envy him. But he was so down-to-earth and charming that everyone found him irresistible. I used to call him the Mayor of Yonkers because it seemed that everywhere he went, everyone knew him.

The timing of his visit was opportune. He also was looking to get into a business and make some real money. But he wanted something legitimate; he was not into drugs. Together we came up with a great idea: We would open an Italian restaurant for lunch and dinner, then turn it into a night club later in the evening, right in Richie's neighborhood. He was such a natural promoter that I was certain he could single-handedly fill the place. I would front the money and Richie would spread the word. A few weeks later we found a rundown Irish pub in the middle of Yonkers that we gutted and transformed into an elegant nightspot. Help came from Richie's family, who all seemed to be contractors, carpenters, and electricians. Whatever we needed materialized on the spot and it came together quickly.

We agreed to call the restaurant "Zook's," after Richie, whose full last name was Zucchero. We opened New Year's Eve of 1976, by invitation only. The place was packed with a young, hip crowd. No one wanted to leave its upbeat, intimate, elegant atmosphere. Everyone praised the food and the décor. At the entrance was a semi-circular mahogany bar that, at 85 feet long, was the largest in all of Westchester. It sat fifty, with standing room for five times that. Above the bar was a mural depicting two lovers embracing in a green forest, which was painted by a young Spanish artist who had worked on it for three months. We hauled in the money. From eight at night until four in the morning people poured in. It seemed like the front door never had a chance to close.

One night while the restaurant was under construction, I got a call from my great friend Willie. Willie had been my student at Taft High in the Bronx. From the beginning we shared a soul connection, as if he were a son of mine from another lifetime. Like me, Willie loved basketball. In high school, he'd looked up to me not only as his teacher and coach but as his mentor. And I was a white guy who could beat him and his friends in basketball.

Willie was excited about a fighter he'd just seen, Marvin Jenkins, a kid from his neighborhood. Marvin was twenty-two years old and undefeated in his first few professional fights. As an amateur, he was one of the few fighters in the world to have beaten the legendary champion "Sugar Ray" Leonard.

"You've got to come with me to see this kid," Willie said. "He's the next champion of the world. And we can get him."

Marvin was having contract problems and was looking for someone he could trust to handle his career. Willie wanted the two of us to be partners in promoting and training Marvin. We watched Marvin fight a kid almost twenty pounds heavier (because his original opponent backed out), and win with impressive ease. We met with him afterward in his dressing room. I liked him immediately.

On the way home, Willie was so excited he could hardly contain himself. He'd always dreamed of working with a world-class athlete and he was convinced that Marvin could be developed into a champion. I shared Willie's fascination with professional boxing, and agreed that Marvin could become truly great.

A week later we signed a contract with Marvin that gave us the exclusive rights to direct his career. I would train Marvin, and together Willie and I would promote him. I needed his parents' approval and support if Marvin was to trust me completely, especially since I was white. We met with them to discuss the changes and sacrifices necessary to make him a champion. They lived in a run-down, rat-infested apartment house in the center of Harlem, at 125th Street and 7th Avenue. The hallways were was so dark it was almost impossible to keep from tripping over the garbage that was everywhere, along with the stench of urine and human waste.

But once inside their apartment I felt better. His family was concerned with and interested in Marvin's future. They asked good questions. I told them that Marvin needed to get out of the neighborhood and get to a place where he could train every day without distractions. I wanted him to stay with my family in the country. We had a huge house and lots of woods and trails he could run on, and I assured them that we would take very good care of him. They were excited by the idea that Marvin could become a world champion, and, of course, bring in a lot of money.

At first Marvin was afraid he'd be lonely without his friends and family, but he finally agreed to move in with us. Very quickly he adjusted to the new situation and while he settled in, I continued working on the restaurant.

One morning, about six months after we opened Zook's, Richie called. Had I seen the papers? I hadn't. He told me that one of our regulars, a girl in her early twenties, had been found shot dead with her boyfriend after leaving our club the night before. They were the latest victims of Son of Sam, who had begun terrorizing the New York area the previous July. Police believed that he lived in Yonkers, not far from our nightclub.

The killings continued for months. The victims were all young lovers parked in their cars late at night. The papers and the media were relentless in their coverage. All over the city most of the clubs catering to young people either closed, or like Zook's, sat empty. This crazed gunman had almost single-handedly shut down the toughest city in the world. Richie and I managed to hang on because of the restaurant trade, even though the bulk of our income had come from the bar and the after-dinner crowd. When I began using my drug money to keep the restaurant alive, I knew we couldn't last much longer.

In July 1977, Son of Sam was finally arrested and all of New

York seemed to relax. As it turned out, he did live in Yonkers, and not far from Zook's. Some of our old nightclub crowd drifted back, but it was clear that business would never be as good as before. We put the place up for sale. For almost a year there was no interest. We were on the verge of going out of business when one day in the fall of 1978 our real estate agent brought a retired police captain to take a look at the club. Within a half hour he said he wanted to buy the place. A month later, the papers were signed and the restaurant was sold.

Meanwhile, Marvin "Kid Harlem" Jenkins remained undefeated and was rising in the world rankings. I had never trained a professional fighter. It was extremely challenging for me to step up to the professional level in a sport that I loved as a spectator but knew little of as an insider or trainer. But I sensed that the relationship itself was more important than any technical skills I might teach him. For anything great to happen, I felt that I first had to earn his respect and trust.

I found a boxing gym owned by the legendary manager/trainer Charlie Casserta, which was in White Plains about twenty minutes from my house in Chappaqua. Charlie was a little old man, almost eighty, who wore a silly-looking toupee and smoked fat cigars that were so big they almost hid his face and impeded his speech. His lips and chin were crusted over by a repulsive dry brown drool. He still had his faculties, although he seemed a bit scrambled as he spoke. If he weren't so famous and so comical-looking, he would have been a disgusting sight.

Charlie had managed and trained fifty-three Golden

Gloves amateur champions over the fifty-plus years he'd been in boxing. He also trained and managed many professional fighters, including several world champions. He was noted for the part he played in the movie "Requiem for a Heavyweight," with Anthony Quinn and Jackie Gleason. Everyone in boxing knew him. He was the kind of personality that made the sport down-to-earth and fun, and the kind of character who made a movie like "Rocky" a classic whether you liked boxing or not. He immediately invited us to come work out at his gym, promised to do whatever he could to get us fights, and even said he would work Marvin's corner.

So we began a training routine. My kids, who loved Marvin, would wake us up at 5:00 a.m. for five miles of road work. Sometimes I would follow him in my car and some days I would run with him. After his run, we'd go to my basement where Marvin worked out for an hour on the heavy bag, speed bag, jump rope, and then finish with shadow boxing. Then I made him breakfast. This was a bit tricky at first, because I wanted him to follow a much more nutritious diet than he was used to. He reluctantly complied, and after a while came to appreciate it. He was afraid that cutting back on his usual heavy meals would reduce his strength and power, but what he found instead was that not only did he feel stronger, but it made it easier for him to keep his weight right where he wanted it at 142 to 145 pounds. It also dramatically improved his hand speed.

After breakfast, we would drive to the gym where he'd go through several hours of intense training, warming up for forty-five minutes with push-ups, sit-ups, stretching, and shadow boxing, then work out on the heavy bag and the speed bag. After moving around the ring, throwing punches and working on combinations, he'd be ready for a sparring session.

In a few months, Marvin was in tremendous condition. He looked fantastic. He dazzled everyone with his workouts. He was so quick that no one could hit him, and he was getting stronger with his punches. He was starting to take on the look of a champ.

Charlie Casserta booked him as the headliner at the Westchester County Center in White Plains, New York, where we could begin to build his career toward a championship. He looked great. The crowds loved him because he was so quick and so colorful. The promoters loved him because he could fight, but even more because he filled the seats in the arena.

We got in touch with Gil Clancy, the matchmaker at Madison Square Garden, the Mecca of boxing. Gil loved Marvin's skill and potential and offered us a fight with the fourth-ranked welterweight in the world, a guy from Puerto Rico. He told us if Marvin won that fight, he would be in line for a shot at the title.

By Autumn of 1978 the stage was set. I was happy – 39 and in my prime. I had a beautiful, loving wife and three great kids living in the house of our dreams. Fame and fortune were within my grasp. Everything was going my way. I knew Kid Harlem would win a championship – he was that good. Life couldn't be better. Once again, I had the world by the tail.

PART II: Freedom

"Peace. It does not mean to be in a place where there is no noise, trouble, or hard work. It means to be in the midst of those things and still be calm in your heart."

- Unknown

Chapter 12:

Busted

I pulled into the stone driveway of our house, shifted into park and, while Ramona and Marvin waited in the car, I got out to check the mailbox. I was full of contentment, savoring the way my life was going. Then out of the dark, I heard the scream:

"Freeze! Police! Freeze!" I looked up to see half a dozen plainclothes and uniformed police emerge from the woods, guns drawn and pointed at me. I turned toward the street, instinctively looking for escape, but before I could take a step, three police cars, lights flashing, moved in and blocked the driveway.

A hard hand grabbed the back of my neck and shoved my face onto the hood of the nearest car. The owner of the hand leaned over me; I could see that his other hand held a gun. "If you so much as breathe the wrong way, punk, I'll splatter your brains all over the hood."

My energy drained away. I leaned helplessly upon the car

as someone jerked my hands behind my back and snapped handcuffs on. The door swung open, and someone pulled me to my feet and threw me into the rear seat. Doors slammed. The car began to pull away.

I heard Ramona screaming. "Wait! Please wait! You must have the wrong person. My husband didn't do anything." She was running toward the car, sobbing. "Please, leave him alone, let him go!" But the officer rolled up his window and kept going, veering sharply out of my driveway.

As we gained speed, I pressed my face against the window and tried to get Ramona's attention, to signal her that everything would be all right. I could only watch, my heart aching, as she raced after the car and then gave up. She stood in the middle of the road, sobbing. That was my last view of her as we rounded a curve in the road.

Of course, she was wrong: I *had* done something, they didn't have the wrong person, and they weren't going to let me go. And then, a block later, the police car pulled over. Both cops turned and looked at me. I was limp with fright. "You are under arrest for the sale of a controlled substance," said the cop in the passenger seat, a Hispanic guy with a real street attitude. "This is an A-1 felony. Under New York State law conviction carries a mandatory life sentence. And we've got the evidence and testimony to convict you."

The cop in the driver's seat, a young red-haired guy with freckles, added, "But it isn't *you* we want. We want your connection. You tell us your source, we'll turn this car around, and you'll sleep in your own bed tonight. Think of your family and your kids."

Even in my terrified state I couldn't force the words out of my mouth. I sat like a stone, staring mutely at the officers. I could feel sweat sliding down my sides.

The cops waited. When it became clear that I had nothing to say, the Hispanic officer shook his head in disgust. "You're going away for life, baby," he snapped. "You blew it. We gave you your chance. We're outta here!"

The freckle-face cop wasn't finished with trying to get me to talk. "C'mon, do you really want to protect your connection?" he said with a wink. "Tell us what we want to know and we'll take you home. If you cooperate, we'll recommend that you don't do time. You'll be protected, and nothing more will happen to you."

I sat frozen. When I was under investigation for stock fraud, and facing little or no jail time, I was grateful for and comfortable about revealing the information the authorities wanted. Now I had so much more to lose, yet I could not open my mouth and save myself. After a few moments, they looked at each other and shrugged. We continued to jail.

At Manhattan South, the Lower East Side precinct near Chinatown, I was fingerprinted, booked, and thrown into a cell that looked like a cage from the Bronx Zoo – the real one, not the comfortable office I had worked in a few years before.

I was locked inside a wire-mesh cage with a man who looked

absolutely insane. He stank, he was disheveled, he coughed, and he never stopped ranting. I stayed as far away from him as I could within the confines of that cage. For five or six dreadful hours I sat in the opposite corner, trying hard to be invisible. It was almost a relief to be hustled into a police van and driven to the notorious Riker's Island. However, over the next three days I learned how well-deserved its reputation is.

I was placed in a holding cell with about twenty other guys still wearing their street clothes. They all looked spaced out; most seemed drunk or drugged. There was no place to sit, so I sat on the cold concrete floor, my back against the wall. In the middle of the cell was a toilet bowl with half a seat, covered with human waste. As if it weren't already disgusting beyond words, an inmate staggered up, bent over and added his spew to the mix. I didn't sleep that night; I was afraid to close my eyes.

Early the next morning, we were escorted to a large, open area, where we were ordered to remove our clothing and place all personal items in the small containers they handed out. I began to empty my pockets. My hand closed around a huge wad of money, and a shock went through me. In the panic of the last twenty-four hours, I had completely forgotten that I had taken payment for a drug deal just hours before my arrest. Now I was getting ready to strip naked in front of jail guards and a group of guys who were capable of God knows what, and I discover I'm carrying five thousand dollars in hundred-dollar bills.

How am I going to explain this? I thought.

I glanced furtively to my right, then to my left, looking for a friendly face – or even a neutral face. Each inmate I glanced at seemed more menacing than the last. Finally, in desperation, I turned to the one closest to me – a guy built like a Kodiak bear – showed him the roll of bills, and blurted out, "What should I do with this?"

He looked at me like I was out of my mind.

"Put it in your sock, you moron," he said.

Hands shaking, I hastily rolled up my pants cuff and stuffed the wad in my sock, then rolled the cuff back down, quickly stood, and slowly undressed. I stood there in my underwear and socks, hoping not to be noticed.

I looked around. We were lined up shoulder to shoulder, face front. Everyone except me was naked. One officer patrolled the line, inspecting everyone from various angles. Another guard finally noticed me. He burst out laughing, stopped everything, and signaled the other officers. They all looked at me – prisoners and guards alike – and roared. I had never felt so embarrassed or vulnerable.

"Now don't be shy, little boy," one guard jeered. "Take the rest of your clothes off for daddy. No one's gonna hurt you."

Slowly I dropped my underpants, trying to keep the roll of bills in my sock positioned at my heel. Another guard sauntered over and peered down at my feet.

"What is *that*?" he said, pointing to the grapefruit-sized lump in my sock. Reaching down, he yanked off the sock, and the roll exploded – fifty hundred-dollar bills scattering around the floor like confetti.

You'd think this was the funniest comedy act they'd ever seen. Guards and prisoners howled and whistled and carried on while I stood in their midst in a state of shock. Finally, the hilarity wound down, the guards restored order and confiscated the cash, we prisoners put our clothes back on and were marched away.

To my surprise, I felt a deep sense of relief that the money was gone. Not a word of the incident was ever brought up again.

At mid-morning, we were led into a huge, dark cellblock. I paused at the threshold. Three levels of cells were ranked on one side, facing a large, open recreation area. The topmost level of cells shared the recreation area's 70-foot ceiling and looked across its cavernous space into dozens of shattered windows. Incongruously, birds zoomed through the upper reaches of this space. They offered no counterpoint to the pandemonium below, however. A few dozen half-naked men – some in street clothes, some in prison garb, some with bandanas around their heads – seemed to be running around, shrieking and screaming. In every corner, TV sets screamed at full volume. It was a scene out of Dante's Inferno, and I was preparing to enter the first circle of Hell.

The gates clanged open. A guard led me through the cellblock and everyone stopped to check me out. I was ushered into a tiny cell at the top level. The heavy door slammed shut.

I looked around. To my right was a short, narrow metal bed with a mattress folded in half, a sheet and a pillowcase. The damp, mildewed mattress stank of urine. To my left was a toilet, which I urgently needed to use. But as I flushed it, the water backed up and spilled over, bringing sewage with it. The water rose, soaking my shoes and my socks. And there was nowhere I could go. All I could do was stand there and stare in helpless disbelief.

I did my best to somehow settle in, and even managed to fall asleep, my head pillowed on my leather jacket, stuffed in the pillowcase. Late that night, a piercing scream shocked me awake. Footsteps thundered up the stairs and approached my cell. In my sleep-hazed brain, I thought they were coming to get me. Then all the cell doors clanged open at once, and a dozen riot-squad officers bolted past my cell. I heard someone shriek, "Cut him down, cut him down!" My twenty-year-old neighbor had hanged himself.

The next morning, a guard came to tell me I had a visitor. Heart pounding, I entered the visiting room, eagerly searching for Ramona's beautiful face. When I found her, I threw my arms around her and held on for dear life, weeping and begging her to get me out of there.

Arms around each other, we stumbled over to a little table and sat down. Ramona tried to talk to me, but I couldn't let her speak. All I was aware of were my needs, my terror, and my anguish. I begged her not to leave me. I wept and I ranted while she tried to calm me down.

"Alan, please, please!" was all she could say. She was embarrassed. She sat with me for an hour, but it seemed like five minutes. I watched helplessly as she disappeared from sight.

A guard escorted me back to my cell. When the door shut

behind me, I looked around and realized that – for the first time in my life – I was totally alone.

The attorney who got me out of Riker's wasn't a criminal lawyer, and when he recommended I retain someone who was (the charge was an A-1 felony that carried a mandatory sentence of fifteen to twenty-five years to life), I readily took his advice. The reality of what I was facing had begun to register. I'd spent only three days in prison, and felt as if I'd been to hell and back. The thought of spending the rest of my life in that world was beyond horrifying. It was easy to see why some prisoners took their own lives.

I had no idea where to start or whom to call. My previous legal problems were inconsequential compared to this. I'd always believed I could wiggle out of any situation, but this time I felt myself spiraling helplessly out of control, trapped in a drama whose conclusion had already been determined.

I called Warren. He'd been raised on the streets of Harlem and had been in and out of trouble himself, so I figured he knew criminal attorneys. To my surprise, he'd already contacted an uncle who was a numbers-runner under indictment in a case involving millions of dollars in cocaine and heroin. Warren said his uncle's lawyer, Steven Benson, was the best, and would no doubt get me off.

I met with the uncle and Steven a few days later at a little place in north Harlem called the Flash Inn – an infamous gathering place for some of Harlem's most notorious organized crime figures. Steven listened attentively as I unfolded the whole story, interrupting from time to time to ask questions. After an hour, he said he thought the police might think they have the upper hand, but we still had plenty of wiggle room. I began to feel confident again.

A week or so later, Steven called and asked me about a guy named Paul Martino. I explained that Paul worked in my restaurant for a while and I had befriended him. He was out to the house often, and enjoyed hanging out and playing with the dogs and the kids, all of whom adored him. He was practically one of the family.

"Did he ever show up with a new girlfriend?" Steven asked.

He had, in August the previous year. We all liked her immediately.

"And did she and Paul buy coke from you?" he asked.

I was beginning to feel that familiar sick feeling in my stomach. At the end of that visit, Paul asked me if I had any coke on hand. I had sold drugs to him in the past, so this was not an unusual request. I got him what he wanted and they left.

"Some friend," Steven said. "Paul was an informer, and his 'girlfriend' was a cop. He set you up."

I began to shake. Once again, someone close to me had betrayed me. It seemed like a familiar scenario. I had a lifetime's worth of disappointed expectations, going all the way back to grammar school: the friends who tattled on me; the times my parents told me that if I just told the truth, I wouldn't be punished, then punished me anyway; the friends, business colleagues, and employees who turned state's evidence against me in the stock fraud investigation. In that moment, I became very paranoid. I felt that I could no longer trust anyone.

I probably shouldn't have been surprised about the bust. My old free-spirited friend, Joey, had been arrested in the fall of 1978, so I knew I was being watched. His arrest panicked me; I buried what was left of my stash in the backyard. It was too little, too late, of course. By that time the police had already executed the sting with Paul's help. They had all they needed to convict me.

A few months later, Steven told me the DA had offered a deal. The DA didn't really want to go to trial. The political return on a small-potatoes guy like me wasn't big enough to justify the expense. At the same time, he couldn't just dismiss the case. Dismissing a case against a drug dealer was just the kind of thing a political rival could leverage into a successful campaign for the DA's seat.

So, in exchange for a guilty plea, he said he would recommend a sentence of only one year. I wouldn't have to give up any names and I'd be eligible for parole in a few months.

While the prospect of prison time still terrified me, this offer looked like good news to me. Maybe there was a way to get out of this mess after all! I began to feel a mixture of relief and excitement. Steven must have seen it on my face.

"Alan," he said, "they're offering this deal because they have no case. Do you think they'd give you this kind of shot if they had a chance of winning?"

My heart fell.

"It's too early to take this deal," he said. "We can beat this thing even if we have to go to trial. But of course, it's up to you."

Up to me? My mind went blank. I had never been in this kind of situation before. I was totally naïve about the way the criminal process worked. I knew nothing about the law. How could I make any kind of intelligent decision?

The internal war started up. Part of me wanted to take the deal and end the nightmare; another part was petrified of going to prison, no matter how short the sentence. Self-pity made a plea: Whatever crime I'd committed, whatever wrongs I'd done, shouldn't what I'd already endured count for something? Would God please forgive me already?

And then there was the part that wanted Steven to feel sorry for me, to see me as a "good" person who got caught up in a "bad" situation so he would be moved to really work hard for me. This part of me was worried about offending him. After all, Steven wouldn't be inclined to put his best efforts into my case if he was upset with me, would he?

In my own mind, Steven was all I had. He was my voice, my only hope for freedom. What he did, what he said in court, how he handled everything, would decide my fate.

I had no choice and no energy to fight this, so I gave up and put my life in his hands, and turned down the DA's deal.

Steven distanced himself from me after that. I heard from

him a few times when he called to say the DA was pushing for me to take the deal. When I asked him what I should do, his answer was always the same.

"Just sit tight and leave everything to me," he'd say.

The trial lasted four days. Helplessly, I watched it unfold as if I were witnessing someone else's nightmare. I waited for Steven to take charge, to say something that would give me hope. He never did. He seemed not to care. I prayed that something or someone would rescue me in the end. I knew I was going down, and I was going to face it alone.

Just before the closing arguments were presented, Steven and I conferred in a little room adjacent to the courtroom. The DA walked in.

"He's guilty!" he growled at Steven, pointing his finger at me. "He has no case! You go back into that courtroom, and he goes away for life. I'm giving you one last chance. Accept the plea bargain now, or I'll withdraw it. That's it. Take it or leave it."

Steven stood, red-faced. He told the DA to do something unprintable with his plea bargain. The DA put up his hands in mock surrender and left without a word.

We marched back into the courtroom and each attorney delivered his summation. The jury went out and returned almost immediately with a verdict of guilty. My attorney stated for the record that we would appeal. But there was no energy, no conviction behind his words.

It was over. I was going to jail.

I was convicted on March 13, 1980. Sentencing was scheduled for sixteen weeks after the verdict. I spent those intervening weeks living inside my head, constantly looking for a thought, a feeling of relief from the fear and pain that wouldn't leave me even for a second.

Ramona and I had been spending most of our time between my arrest and the trial in Greenburg, NY at the house of our closest friends, Nan and Michael, and we continued this pattern now.

We would all sit around and talk, trying to rationalize the situation, trying to fill each other with hope. Most of the conversation was centered on trying to pick up my spirits, trying to find positive ways to see the outcome. For me, there was only the sense of impending doom. The only relief I found was in getting stoned or drunk every day.

We would drink Stolichnaya gimlets, smoke some pot and then go out to a restaurant and overeat. Many nights Ramona and I never even went home. We would sleep over at Nan and Michael's house, get up the next day, and do it all over again.

My whole lifestyle had fallen apart. I had completely stopped exercising. I drank more than I ever had. I put on weight. I didn't care how I looked anymore. In my attempt to numb my emotions with drugs, alcohol, and food, I had somehow almost lost my will to live. It was like I was trying to kill myself slowly, or to look so bad that somehow the universe would take pity on me and stop the torture. As the trial date had drawn closer and closer, my whole being had shut down to a point where I saw only pain and fear.

The one amazing part of this whole process, however, was that I had a part of me that every once in a while would break through the darkness and pain and get me to stand up, to have hope, to want to continue. It seemed to come up in my darkest moments, when there seemed to be no hope, and get me to want to fight. It would have been very easy just to completely give up at that time, and most of me had, but there was a deeper part of me that never did, that kept me going and wouldn't let me quit on myself.

The memory of my last night at home will always be with me. Ramona was in complete denial. I had been convicted of an A-1 felony, which carried a mandatory sentence of 15 to 25 years to life. But Ramona kept trying to reassure me that the judge would somehow not put me behind bars. She couldn't accept the fact that he had no discretion, and I had neither the strength nor the desire to fracture her illusion. In a strange way, her naïve faith gave me some hope.

I fell asleep that night in her arms, holding onto her, desperate to find a place of safety. She murmured over and over, "You're not going to prison, you're not going to prison. Stop thinking that way or it will come true." She repeated it like a mantra, all night long.

I woke the next morning encompassed in a darkness that

was almost palpable. The feeling intensified as we pulled out of the driveway. I looked back at the house and felt sure I would never see it again.

I had dressed for the courthouse in a suit and tie. Steven had told me to bring a toothbrush and change of clothes, just in case I wouldn't be going home. He planned to ask for a continuance of my bail while we appealed the verdict, but said there was a good chance the judge would not grant it. Sitting beside me, Ramona again told me with complete confidence not to worry, that I'd be home that evening with her and the children.

Steven never showed up. Instead, he sent an associate, a kid who looked like he was still in law school. I couldn't believe it. I sat on a bench at the back of the courtroom, head in hands, inconsolable. My lawyer had placed my fate in the hands of a novice.

My case number was called. As I was ushered down the aisle to face the judge, I glanced around. A couple dozen close friends and relatives huddled in the back, trying to look hopeful and failing miserably. Except Ramona. Her smile lit up the room. She could have been waiting for a table at her favorite restaurant; she was unconcerned. In that moment she gave me strength; in that moment there was no separation between us – just love!

The young attorney did his best, making a passionate plea on my behalf, but he didn't have much to work with. The decision was out of his hands. He finished and sat down. The judge asked me if I had anything to say. I stood there, my head bowed, speechless. The judge said that what I had done was unforgivable, that there could never be any justification for selling drugs, and I deserved to spend time in prison for it. He suggested I use the time to reflect on my actions.

"If I had discretion in this case, I would not impose the mandatory sentence," he said. Then he looked me in the eye and intoned, "I have no choice in this matter but to sentence you, Alan Gompers, to fifteen years to life."

My sister-in-law screamed in grief. As a guard handcuffed me and led me out of the courtroom, I took one last look at my stunned family. Incredibly, my dear Ramona's serene expression hadn't changed. Our eyes met and she mouthed the words, "Don't worry, I love you! Stay strong!"

The door opened, the guard pushed me through, and I took my first steps toward hell.

Why didn't I cooperate with the police? It would have been so simple to speak a name and get myself out of this awful bind. The only thought I remember having at the time was that if I gave them a name, if I did what they were asking me to do, something terrible would happen to me. But that doesn't really explain my silence.

The answer to the question is in two parts. The first part had to do with Joey's arrest. He had been picked up about five months before for the same A-1 felony, and was offered the same deal: Give up the name of your supplier and you won't do any time.

Without hesitation, he flatly turned the offer down. He told the police, his lawyer, and me that he would never give anyone up, that he was no rat, and that he would rather spend the rest of his life in jail than give up a name. He said he did what he did and he would take his chances with whatever his lawyer worked out.

Joey was dead serious. I couldn't even begin to fathom that he was willing to give up his whole life for some silly principle. I tried to get him to give the police a name, but there was no reasoning with him. He just looked me in the eyes and said, with absolute conviction and finality, that if he did give someone up, he would never feel good about himself again.

I had never heard him say anything with that much certainty. Even though I thought he was insane, I couldn't help but wonder where he got the strength and guts to put his life on the line that way. I didn't understand why he did what he did, but a part of me was deeply moved.

So when it came to me to make the same choice, Joey's example had settled deep into my being and made it impossible for me to save myself.

I am so grateful I didn't. It was one of the few times in my life that I had experienced what it was to be true to myself, and to actually feel what it was like to have real courage and faith. I now know that I am the creator of everything that happens to me, that no one else is ever responsible for my pain and suffering, and that I must take responsibility for my own actions. I didn't know any of this at the time, but my decision was no small thing. That moment ultimately made me feel better about myself than

I ever had before.

But there is a second, deeper part of the answer that I only came to understand much later: Fate. I was not supposed to get out of this predicament. The bust was a divine set-up. I had always thought I was clever enough to get myself out of any situation. I had no humility. I could never see how pain and suffering, failure and unhappiness came into my life. I was always too busy in my mind, trying to manipulate the situation rather than look at what I was doing to create it. This bust took away all my options and put me in a situation that – for the first time in my life – I couldn't get out of and had no control over. That short-circuiting of my ego left me open and vulnerable. Being open and vulnerable let me know that I couldn't do anything, that nothing I could do or say could change anything.

Looking back on the bust more than 25 years later, I now can say with certainty:

It was God's grace, in that police car. I sat in the car, unable to open my mouth, because God wouldn't let me. It's as simple as that.

Chapter 13:

Sing Sing

The next three months were a nightmare. With my exit from the courtroom, I began a process the New York State prison system calls – with the utter lack of irony only a government bureaucracy can pull off – "reception." To this day, whenever I receive an invitation for a reception, I always think of the contrast in experiences.

A sort of long-term, traveling reception began at Downstate Correctional Facility in Fishkill, New York, about an hour north of New York City. Upon my arrival, I was issued the standard light brown uniform and assigned to a cellblock with two dozen other inmates. Next morning, we were herded to the prison barbershop and relieved of our hair, then over to a huge gang shower where I was handed a small squeeze bottle filled with a disinfectant and ordered to wash. The stuff was a nauseating greenish-brown and no doubt had been created to kill any bugs prisoners might bring in. It scorched my skin, especially the more tender parts. While those chemicals accomplished their intention, they also scorched the tender remnants of my sense of self-worth.

For the next few weeks, I was shuttled from one department to another, for round after round of evaluations. One of my worst experiences was the chest x-ray. By the time I was called I'd worked myself into a lather. I had always been afraid of hospitals and medical procedures, and during the hour-long wait I convinced myself they were going to find some horrible lung disease and send me to the prison hospital to perform a painful, invasive surgical procedure against my will. Even if my lungs turned out to be fine, I was sure the harmful effects of the x-rays themselves would hasten my death in the future.

When the technician called my name, I flat-out refused to cooperate. I lacked the strength to fight the technician, who was at least twice my size, but fortunately he was a decent guy. He was gentle and kind, He explained that it would be all over quickly, that I had nothing to worry about. I was relieved when it was over, but was still afraid that something would happen to me from the x-rays.

I remember this period vividly: the rancid smell, the authoritarian arrogance of most of the staff, my feelings of helplessness. It all felt so inhumane, so unnatural and insensitive. Day after day, I submitted to routine physical and medical exams, and I completed written evaluations, like the standardized tests we took in school, to determine my intelligence and identify any psychological aberrations I might harbor. The evaluations and tests are supposed to help the Department of Corrections determine the kinds of jobs an inmate is qualified to do, and whether you should do your time in minimum, medium, or maximum security. In my case there was no need for assessment – the nature of my crime made it mandatory that I serve my sentence in a maximum-security facility.

Six weeks of this exhausting routine, and then the order came to pack up again. I was being sent further upstate to another "reception center" to receive my inmate number, and for further processing before being moved to my final destination. This reception center was one of the most infamous maximum-security prisons in the world: Sing Sing.

Sing Sing is literally "up the river," located along the Hudson outside Ossining, New York. Along with a dozen other prisoners, I arrived in a prison bus handcuffed to the seat in front of me and shackled at the feet. We were led through two huge steel gates into a large open area. There was tremendous tension in the air. The pressure behind the walls was palpable. I was escorted to a housing unit and assigned a cell.

The next day, we were taken through orientation. The guard who processed my paperwork was obese, sweaty, and nasty looking. Everything about him seemed dirty, unhealthy and mean. As he shuffled the papers of the inmates, he seemed to relish wielding his power over each one.

In time, I came to understand that the way he looked and acted was simply a projection onto the inmates of all the unhappiness and venom he had accumulated within himself. I just happened to be in his way at the time; it had nothing to do with me. But that day, all I could do was react. He finished with my papers and looked up with a malicious grin. I stared into his cold eyes, sensing the pleasure he took in hurting and intimidating me. "You're mine now," he said. "Your new name is 80A-2139, and your ass belongs to me. As a Lifer, you have no rights. In the eyes of the State, you are dead. And wherever you go for the rest of your life, even if someday you manage to get out of this joint, you'll never be able to get rid of that stink."

80A-2139.

That number signaled the end of my identity as a citizen and a human being. It stripped away the final shreds of any self-worth I still might have retained and obliterated my connection to the outside world.

When I first arrived at Sing Sing, it had the notorious distinction of being one of the most dangerous facilities in the system. Inmates in my cellblock looked especially threatening and unpredictable, and I remember walking around the corridors feeling extremely paranoid, constantly looking over my shoulder. There was always something going down. Tension and pressure was always at a peak. Fights broke out everywhere with regularity.

To help reduce the tension, the administration turned the prison chapel into a movie theater on weekends. This gave a thousand inmates an opportunity to get out of their cells for a few hours. One Sunday, shortly after the lights went out there was a scream, then a lot of yelling and frenzied commotion. The lights snapped back on, the doors flew open, and "The Goon Squad" (guards armed with both guns and clubs) stormed the room. A few minutes later they carried out a stretcher bearing a body with multiple stab wounds. He was dead before they could get him to the prison infirmary.

This was the first time I had witnessed a murder. The tragedy confirmed my greatest fear of being in prison. My expectations about prison life, which were hyped by the media and by my conditioning, suddenly were validated. Having seen the violence in the movie theater, I was faced with the realization that my own cellblock was a rogues gallery of violent inmates who had been in prison most of their lives and had nothing to lose. I was afraid to leave my cell and stayed inside as much as possible. Nevertheless, three times a day the doors clanged open and everyone had to move out "into population." I had no choice.

One morning the doors opened and the block came alive. An inmate known as Iron Man swaggered into my cell. This was an outrageous violation of the unspoken rule that no one enters another man's "house" without permission.

I'd heard about Iron Man. He'd spent most of his life pumping iron. He was massive, maybe 300 pounds on a five-foot-four-inch frame. If his body was made of iron, his face was made of stone. There was not a hint of softness about him. And here he stood, looming over me as I sat on the toilet. He towered over me, his body almost touching mine. I was afraid to speak or move.

122 ❖ Maximum Security

The hair stood up on my arms when he softly said, "I understand this is your first time in prison. This is a dangerous, dangerous place. New guys like you need protection, someone like a big brother to watch out for you." There are lots of guys, Iron Man explained, who have nothing to lose and would just as soon "turn you out in a heartbeat," (that is, rape me, then make me his sex slave). But if I would "do the right thing" (that is, let him have his way with me) he would make sure I was protected.

He gazed significantly at my crotch, then cradled his own. "You get what I'm sayin', man?" he crooned ominously, almost as if he were speaking from some other place and time. Without saying anything overtly threatening, he was eerie and threatening. I felt bile rise in my throat. Iron Man smiled dreamily. "I'll be back, man," he said. Then he was gone.

I felt utterly helpless. Nothing in my life had prepared me to deal with someone like Iron Man. But a part of me kept saying, *I can't let this happen; I will not let this happen.* I didn't know how I was going to prevent it, but I knew *some how, some way,* I had to.

For the next several days I lived in terror, unable to eat or sleep, watching for Iron Man but unable to think what I would do if I saw him. One afternoon in the yard, standing as inconspicuously as possible in a remote corner and looking nervously around for my would-be tormentor, I thought I saw my old friend Joey, and my heart leapt. Could it be? I inched closer for a better look, hoping that it was him. And it was. I ran to him.

After we hugged, Joey stood back and looked me over. "Alan, what's wrong?" he cried. "I hardly recognized you. You look terrible!"

It was all I could do to keep from breaking into sobs. I hated how I felt, and despised myself for being so weak and pitiful. Joey listened intently as I poured out the story of Iron Man. When I was finished, he looked at me squarely and said, "Okay. Go back to your cell, lock in, get a good night's rest, and meet me here tomorrow. And don't worry! This situation" he tapped me lightly on the chest with a knuckle to punctuate his words, "*will be handled.*"

I was astonished at his strength and confidence. He seemed so grounded. I would have given anything, **ANYTHING,** to feel like that.

The next day I returned to the yard and found Joey standing in the same place as before. "Alan, I'd like you to meet Beaver," he said.

Beaver stood about six feet two and 220 pounds. He was neither fat nor muscular, just big and imposing. You could sense he didn't need to prove himself; his mere presence commanded respect.

I found out later that he'd done all his proving on the street, running drugs and numbers. Out there, he was extremely violent, a known assassin who would take a guy out without a second thought. But he had spent most of his adult life in prison. He was ruled to be a persistent felony offender and given a life sentence.

Now in his mid-forties, he was no longer a ticking bomb waiting to explode. He had made his "bones" out in the world and was now able to live off his reputation. Having earned his respect, he in fact was well liked, even admired. He was always nice to me and seemed concerned that I get along all right. I came to like him.

Joey asked me to tell Beaver my story. As I began to recount the details, he interrupted me. "Point this guy out," he said.

Casually, pretending not to look around the yard, I spotted Iron Man. Turning back to Beaver, I indicated with slight movements of my eyes and head where he was standing. Dear God, I thought, please don't let him catch me doing this.

At once Beaver strode over to Iron Man. My heart raced. I held my breath while they spoke. When they both turned and headed over, I had an urge to run, but there was nowhere to go. Then, to my complete amazement, Iron Man walked up to me and stuck out his hand.

"Hey, man!" he said with a big smile. "It's over! I didn't know you knew my man, Beaver." He assured me that I didn't have to worry about him anymore. In fact, he said, "From now on, I've got your back." I must have thanked them a hundred times.

Flooded with relief, I headed back to my cell. As I sat on my bed, mulling over these events, I began to get frightened all over again. I realized how vulnerable and dependent I was, with no idea how to handle myself. I had a sentence of fifteen-to-life. Soon I would be sent to another maximum-security prison, further upstate, "in population" with inmates who were all doing big time and, as Iron Man had said, didn't have a lot to lose. What would happen to me next time I was faced with a similar situation, with no one there to protect me?

At that moment I realized I could not depend on anyone or anything to bail me out. I saw vividly how my fear set me up for others to pick up on immediately. I was projecting it and every inmate would know it, just as Iron Man knew it. My fear not only left me open, it made me a target. I was creating the very situation I feared most.

I had to find some way to overcome my fear. Concealing it wasn't an option. Hiding in my cell was not the answer either. Somehow, I had to find strength and resolve within myself. I had to come out and face my fear, because no matter how much I tried to hide it, *they knew*. They always knew. It wasn't what I said or did, it was about what was going on inside of me, what I was truly feeling, that exposed me. In the end, it was my fear alone that had drawn every predator that crossed my path, like a mosquito to blood.

From that point on, I forced myself to leave my cell every day and move around the prison openly. I sought out situations where I felt more secure and at ease, where I sensed I could fit in. I looked for other inmates who appeared lighter, more open and friendly.

I started playing in some of the pick-up basketball games in the prison yard. The younger guys immediately started calling me "The Old Man" or "Pops." At first they were being derogatory, but as they got to know me, they started to sound almost affectionate. Maybe it was because I was over forty and could still hold my own on the court, or maybe it was because I was the only white guy out there who thought he was good enough to play them. Whatever it was, I was grateful that they accepted me.

It wasn't easy to push myself out of my cell each day. But slowly, over time, my intimidation was replaced by greater confidence. It was nothing dramatic; I was dealing with my fear by facing the world head-on again. I began to relax a little, and that in itself was an incredible relief.

[Not long after I left Sing Sing, these same inmates overran my former cellblock, seized about twenty hostages, and took over the prison. The National Guard was called in and it took over two weeks to restore order. To this day, it remains one of the most dramatic incidents in prison history.]

In September, 1980, I was ordered to pack up for the last time. I was headed for a maximum-security prison in the Catskill Mountains called Eastern New York Correctional Facility. Eastern was only a two-hour drive from the City, but I felt I was leaving the world I knew for another planet.

I was startled by my first look at my new home. I expected the gun towers and the imposing walls, but not the elegant castle-like structure that appeared before me. I relaxed. There was something serene and safe about this red brick building. It looked like it might have been a monastery or a spiritual retreat, not a facility for housing violent criminals.

That impression was cancelled the moment I walked through the gates and onto the guardroom floor, which represented the transition between the free world and the most secure part of the facility. The breeze and the tall trees were replaced with cold steel, large empty rooms, and enormous steel gates. Sitting there, handcuffed and shackled, I shook from intense fear and cold for three long hours, until an escort arrived to take me to my cellblock.

Finally they came to get me. They removed the handcuffs and shackles. We headed toward a cellblock at the rear of the prison. In the dark corridor, blind and cold, I felt as though death and eternity had merged to encompass me.

We entered a huge cellblock, climbed three flights to the top level, and turned down a dimly lit corridor. The block was silent except for snoring noises muffled by the thirty-six steel doors that each locked a man in a six-by-nine cell.

In the shadows about halfway down the corridor, a huge figure loomed. A guard muttered "What's Bigfoot doing out of his cell at this hour?"

"Someone got piped," the other guard said. "It was a mess – blood all over the place. He's just cleaning up."

I'd never seen anything like Bigfoot before. He was close to seven feet tall, and must have weighed well over 350 pounds. As we got closer, I saw that he had a lion's mane of reddish-brown hair that shot out wildly from his head and fell well below his waist. His beard, equally wild, covered his chest. He was barefoot and shirtless. He stared intently at me, eyes glistening.

He didn't look human – he looked insane, ready to attack. The guards slowed down as we got close. I had seen enough; I looked straight ahead, too scared to think.

"Hello, Harry," said one of the guards.

I glanced up. Harry nodded without taking his eyes off me. As we passed, I could hear him breathing heavily and grunting.

We stopped at a cell further down the corridor. One of the guards took out a great ring of keys. He unlocked the door. It swung open and I was pushed inside. It slammed shut. I heard the lock engage. I was alone.

For a few seconds I stood with my back to the door. When I turned, it was all I could do to keep from screaming: Filling the ten-inch-square opening in the door, was Bigfoot's gigantic, disembodied head. Expressionless and motionless, he stared at me. I froze and stared back.

Suddenly he began to laugh and scream and howl, and then he was gone. My thundering heart slowly returned to normal. But before I could catch my breath, he returned, raging and screaming, sticking out his tongue and making faces. Then he vanished again.

I fell to my knees, exhausted. In that moment, I realized that everything in my life was gone. Ramona, on her own for the first time, had panicked and was now with another man. My business had collapsed and most of my money was gone. Friends, family, my children – all seemed part of a different lifetime.

There was nowhere to go, nothing I could do. I searched for a thought, an idea, anything that might offer hope. All I could touch were loneliness and fear – and they were screaming in me with such intensity that, had I died right there, I would have considered it a gift of mercy.

Chapter 14:

Shaktipat

I fell asleep just before the horn sounded for wake-up. For a split second, I was unaware of where I was, and there was no fear or pain, just disorientation. But the minute my mind became active, I felt the knot in my stomach and the sickly fear that always accompanied it.

I stumbled through "chow," unable to eat, and out into the yard in a daze. I was in population, mixing with the other inmates for the first time. In spite of some progress in dealing with my fears at Sing Sing, I still was not jail-wise. I stood there paralyzed, and looked around. I was scared to death.

The yard was huge, probably four to five acres, with a running track, two regulation baseball diamonds, several tennis courts, two full-court basketball courts, four handball and racquetball courts, and two areas set up for soccer and football. At a far corner was a modern-looking chapel that resembled a Japanese pagoda. At the opposite end was the gym building with its weight room, basketball court, boxing ring, track, bleachers that sat over five hundred people, and a shower room.

There were inmates lifting weights and others were playing cards, dominoes, or chess. Groups huddled around several outdoor TV sets screaming obscenities as they watched a football game. Some men lay on the patchy grass taking in the sunshine or watching joggers circle the track.

At the front of the yard the administration building housed the security officers who watched the yard. Surrounding the whole complex was a huge concrete wall with four equidistant gun towers on top. If it weren't for the wall and the gun towers – and the fear in my gut – I could have mistaken this scene for a peaceful public park.

In a small space in front of the entrance to the main yard, several inmates were kneeling, planting flowers. I was shocked. The last thing I expected to see in this godforsaken place was the delicate beauty of flowers. Gazing at them, I felt my heart swell as if I were being reunited with a lost love. It had been months since I'd seen green grass or a flower; it felt like years. I can't even begin to describe how grateful I felt. They were a refuge, symbols of hope and sanctuary. I made my way over to the flowers and stood there, mesmerized. I wanted to touch them, to smell them, to get lost in them, wishing somehow that they could protect me.

I dropped to my knees and lowered my head to take in their fragrance. At the same time I became acutely aware of a knot of pure fear in my gut. This knot had been with me all my life; now I felt it begin to move up into my chest. My body began to heat up. My eyes burned like coals.

Oh no! I thought. *Do NOT break down. Not here!*

I glanced around in a panic and saw the track. I walked toward it, then broke into a run. The tears practically exploded out of my eyes; they poured uncontrollably down my face. I ran past inmates and guards. I ran and I cried. I cried and I ran. It no longer mattered who saw me. I was beyond control.

Within fifteen minutes the tears just stopped. I was depleted, physically and emotionally, and all I wanted was to go off somewhere and be alone. I found a remote corner and sat on the ground with my back against a cement wall. When I looked up, what I saw brought my whole being to a halt. There, rising beyond the walls of the prison, high over the gun towers, were the most majestic, lush, green mountains I had ever seen: the magnificent Shawagunk Mountain Ridge. I felt as if it were reaching out, embracing me, and calming me.

I went back to those times as a little boy when I'd felt so alone and afraid, and the only person who could take away those horrible feelings was my mother. As if by magic, she could always sense my despair and show up when I most needed her. She would put her arms around me, pull me close and whisper into my ear, "It's all right, Alan. Mommy's here. Everything is all right. Don't be afraid." I would be comforted by her warmth and the strength of her love. This experience filled me again, only now I was sitting in a prison yard, almost forty years later, looking out at the mountains. My eyelids became heavy, fluttered and closed. Automatically, I crossed my legs. And I entered into what I now know was a deep state of meditation.

Of course, I had no idea then what I was doing. I had never meditated before. I didn't know what meditation was. I sat there with my eyes closed, resting, thinking nothing, for probably thirty minutes or so. Then, my eyes opened again, on their own.

I blinked and gazed around, stunned. It seemed I'd awakened into a Walt Disney fantasyland. The grim prison yard was transformed, as if someone had taken a magic scrub brush to each molecule of air, each dust mote, each particle of granite and brick so it sparkled like crystal. Everything looked enchanted. Golden rays of sunlight seemed to take personal delight in bouncing off the gun towers and the heads of inmates walking around the yard. The colors looked like none I had ever seen – not just blue, or green, or gray, but some celestial variety of blue and green and gray that made my memory of the "real thing" seem pale and anemic. Wherever I looked, I saw beauty – spectacular, dazzling, exquisite beauty – and all of it seemed infused with joy and an immense, powerful love.

Gradually I became aware of my body and a vague impression that something was missing. I thought about it for a few minutes, then I realized what it was – the knot of fear in my stomach was gone! In the place where it had been for so long, there was now empty space, out of which came wave after wave of contentment, and feelings of lightness so exquisite that I felt as if I could literally lift myself right off the ground.

I let out a sigh. *Dear God,* I thought, *if You really exist, if You can hear me, just let me stay where I am and allow me to hold on to these incredible feelings, and I will never ask You for anything else again.*

After a few minutes, the intensity of the feelings mellowed a bit, although I was still high as a kite. I set off for my cell, wondering what had happened to me – and how I could make it happen again. As I entered my cellblock, I stopped to read a flyer on the community bulletin board. It described a meditation program scheduled for the end of the week in the recreation area.

Meditation? I thought. Was that what I was doing?

I had always thought meditation was weird, and only weirdos practiced it. I also thought that those who meditated were intellectuals who somehow knew more than other people. Especially me. I was intimidated by the practice and by the people who lived in that world and were able to talk about it so glibly. I avoided them so they wouldn't expose my insecurity.

I kept reading until I got to a picture of an Indian meditation master at the bottom of the page. I looked into his laughing, compassionate eyes, and my knees went weak. The contentment and peace of my experience in the yard began to resurface. I knew that what had happened had to do with meditation, and that I was on to something profound. Something had shifted inside me for good.

When I walked into my cell I felt jarred. I felt so pure and so light – and every surface of my cell was covered in years of sticky grime! The floor was covered with a thick layer of dirt and grease. The walls were filthy with huge holes in the plaster and repulsive-looking paint peeling from them. The window was so black that you could barely see outside. The toilet-bowl-and-sink combination was so foul you couldn't tell that it was stainless steel, and its stench made me gag. Just walking into that scene after my experience in the yard hurled me back into a depression.

But now I had a new perspective and I didn't want anything to soil it. I felt a strong desire to only be around things that were clean. Armed with a beat-up old brush that I found in the corner of the cell, some prison-issue soap, and a roll of toilet paper, I got down on my hands and knees and attacked the floor with gusto. As I worked, my spirits began to lift and I was filled with energy. I forgot about my depression, my loneliness, my life sentence, and all the rest of my problems. It was just me and that floor. And slowly, as I began to break through layers of grime, I felt as if I were breaking through lifetimes of obstacles and darkness.

I didn't stop until the floor was so clean and bright that I could feel at ease walking on it in bare feet. When I finished the floor, I began knocking all the curled-up paint off the walls and scrubbing them down. The paint chips fell onto the clean floor, but I didn't care. I wasn't about to let anything mess up the floor for too long anymore.

And it wasn't like I was short on time. At first, that bizarre thought made me laugh, but then a feeling of contentment and well-being began to wash over me. I didn't have to be anywhere! I didn't have to do anything other than what I was doing! In my frenetic life in the world where time was always running out, I had never experienced such an expansive sense of time.

When I was done with the walls, I went to work on the window, then the toilet and sink. I even scrubbed the metal frame of my bed and the small metal desk and chair.

It took several days, but when I was done, everything looked different. I felt a little self-conscious about how clean my cell was because it stood out in sharp contrast from the rest of the cells in the block. The toilet and sink were now shining so brightly I could almost see my reflection. The window was so clean that the glass seemed to disappear. Now I could look out at the breathtaking view of the mountains that rolled off as far as I could see. When I stood in front of the window and gazed out through the bars, they didn't bother me so much anymore. I reveled in a sweet feeling of good fortune, grateful for this special gift of a view – a gift I never would have taken the time to appreciate when I was out in the world.

One morning several days later, the doors to all the cells opened and we were ordered out for our weekly housekeeping assignments around the cellblock – mopping floors, cleaning sinks, and so on. We were allowed to use the time and supplies to tend to our own cells too. While we were working, we were free to walk around the block. It was a nice change of pace from being locked up all the time, even though the cellblock was small.

I was polishing my window with some toilet paper when another inmate peered in, astonished. "Man, are you crazy?" he said. "What you doin' cleaning that window? It don't belong to you. That's state property, man. That ain't your house. You don't go cleanin' state property. You out of your mind?"

I told him I didn't look at it that way, that I just wanted to be comfortable.

"You in jail, bro," he said. "You ain't s'posed to be comfortable. You ain't s'posed to be happy. You *s'posed* to be miserable. What's wrong with you?"

I had the presence of mind not to laugh out loud. I shrugged. He ambled off, shaking his head.

Word got around about Gompers' cell. Each time the cell doors were opened and we were allowed out onto the cellblock floor, another man would come by to check out my "house." Some of the guys liked the idea and began to clean up their cells, too. A few even got into decorating them. After a while, there were cells with carpeting on the floor, rugs on the walls, pictures and posters, hanging beads, and colored lights instead of the standard-issue yellow bulbs. Where they got all this stuff was beyond me, but the wonderful part was that everyone seemed to become a little lighter, a little friendlier, less wary of one another and a little happier with themselves. Even the officer in charge of the block seemed to lighten up.

After my experience in the yard, for the next few months everything I did came from a drive to find out what had happened to me and how I could recreate it. I read everything I could get my hands on, starting with the first book that I came across: the Bible. I don't know whether every cell came with a Bible, but mine did. I had never had any desire to read scripture before, but now I fell on the pages of my King James translation, starved for spiritual wisdom.

The Bible had always seemed to me a lot of fairy tales and nonsense, especially the words of Jesus. My religious upbringing had taught me to see Jesus as belonging to other religions. Many non-Jews who crossed my path said that Jews had betrayed Him, and were ultimately responsible for His death. But the Bible said Jesus was a Jew, that He died a Jew, and that His mother, father and disciples were all Jewish. This made everything all the more confusing.

I had read the New Testament for a college course, but now as I read it, I began to see meaning in His words. It was as if I were reading the Bible for the first time. The words hadn't changed, of course, but I had. I could feel His power and began to understand the greatness in His message. Jesus's teachings began to build a foundation from which I eventually could measure all other wisdom. His words became on-going contemplations that shook my world and gave me a powerful new perspective, a view of reality through the eyes of an enlightened master. During this period, an old friend visited me and told me she thought I had become a "Jesus freak." The truth was that I had become a Truth freak, a Love freak, a Wisdom freak.

Reading the words of Jesus in the Bible was a true revelation, and I received much inner wisdom and experience from His teachings. But a very clear prompting from within encouraged me to continue searching. I sensed deeply that there was something or someone I needed to find that would answer all my questions. Things seemed to be happening on their own. It was as if I didn't have a choice and I was being swept along, but I was not frightened. My experience was one of intense fascination and exhilaration.

One day, I received a visit from my friend Susan, who brought me the book *Be Here Now*. She told me it had been written by an infamous Harvard professor, Richard Alpert, who, along with a fellow professor, Timothy Leary, had been dismissed from the university because of a scandal over their use and distribution to the students of the drug LSD. Susan couldn't stop talking about the power of the book and how it made her think of me when she read it.

When I got back to my cell I began reading it. It was everything she said it was and more. I couldn't put it down. It was the first book on spirituality I had ever read. It was an account of Richard Alpert's experience with LSD at Harvard, being dismissed, then venturing to India in search of a spiritual Master who could guide him on his quest for The Truth. After meeting the great Master Neem Karoli Baba, he had a profound spiritual awakening that I saw immediately was very similar to mine. After living with his Master for some time, he took on the name Ram Dass, came back to America and became a great teacher and guide himself.

I loved the book very much and went on to read several other books he had written. But after some time, I again felt the need to move on. I came across the writing of Alan Watts, a great Zen Buddhist, whose amazing creativity and wisdom captured my fascination. He filled me with insight and helped me to understand things that I never would have been even interested in before.

Next, I came across one of the most powerful books I ever read, *The Autobiography of a Yogi* by Parmahansa Yogananda. Yogananda's journey was so profound, so amazing, that it has to be read to be fully appreciated and experienced. I have no words to describe the energy, power and mystery of his journey. At times it read almost like a fairy tale or myth, but I always experienced that there was nothing fictional in any of it. It was all true. It was four or five hundred pages, written in small print, yet I read it as slowly as I could, because I never wanted it to end. From there I moved on to many of the books of the great spiritual scientist, Krishnamurti. Then I read most of Herman Hesse's books, including his great story *Siddhartha*, about the Indian prince who ultimately attained Enlightenment and became known as "The Buddha."

These were all great books that filled me with awe and insight, yet I kept looking. I deeply, passionately *needed* to understand what had happened to me in the yard. Never before had I given more energy and enthusiasm to anything in my life. I was driven and inspired by an invisible force that filled me with a longing and sense of purpose beyond anything I had ever known.

Chapter 15:

Muktananda

This period of intense reading and searching went on for about six months after I received my spiritual awakening out in the prison yard. Then one morning, as I returned to my cell after a meditation session out in the prison yard, one of the inmates from my cell block came over to my cell and handed me a book.

"Hey, man! I saw you out in the yard yesterday, and I know what you were doing," he said. "Check this out."

I took the book he handed me and found myself gazing into the eyes of the same man whose face appeared on the flyer – an Indian meditation master named Swami Muktananda. Affectionately known as Baba, he was revered as a holy man. The book was his spiritual autobiography, *Play of Consciousness*. Again my knees went weak, and the extraordinary experience I'd had in the yard happened again. Only this time, it was even more powerful. Overwhelmed, I sat down on my bed and began to read.

I'd never encountered such a book in all my life. Every sentence, every word – even the punctuation marks – were filled with such power and wisdom that I immediately knew, without any doubt, that this was the Truth. I couldn't explain how I knew it, I just did. I wanted to drink every word into the emptiness and longings of my heart.

Swami Muktananda's book gave me an explanation for what had happened out in the yard. I had experienced an ancient form of spiritual awakening that is known in all great spiritual traditions. Indian yogis call this awakening *shaktipat*, the descent of Grace. *Shaktipat* awakens what is known as the *kundalini,* a divine energy lying dormant at the base of the spine in all human beings. It begins a process of transformation and purification that leads seekers to self-realization, enlightenment, true liberation. Since the dawn of time, this gift has been handed down from master to disciple.

[The ideas and teachings that I attribute to Swami Muktananda throughout this book are simply my best recollection and understanding of what he said and meant to convey. Muktananda's words and the Siddha Yoga teachings have been the greatest inspiration and support on my journey through life. Hopefully my story will inspire you to go directly to the Siddha Yoga books and take in their timeless wisdom for yourselves.]

I learned that once the awakening occurs, a meditation practice deepens the experience and brings the seeker back to that state. And meditation isn't simply sitting down, crossing your legs, and closing your eyes – it's a *state of being* that does not have to end when you open your eyes and stand up. There is no need to leave the meditative state; we can live from this state – every moment, every second.

Baba explained that the purpose of human life is to experience the Inner Self – not the self we think we are, but the Self that is the experience of God within us. We are designed to merge forever into this state. This state *is* who we really are, and until we merge completely into it, we will find ourselves without true meaning in our lives.

I began to see that what we are looking for cannot be found outside ourselves, because nothing "out there" lasts. Everything is always changing. We might have possessions, money, the perfect marriage, a powerful career, a life full of awards and trophies to mark our accomplishments, but even as we hold these things in our hands, they are dissolving. Our very physical existence is ephemeral. And in the end, the world "betrays" us. In fact, this very betrayal is a form of grace, because it will force us to turn to God.

I learned from this book that every human who seeks, as I did in my lifelong search for approval and security, is actually seeking the Inner Self. We lose touch with it, despite its constant presence, but it is the one thing that is forever stable and reliable, beyond death or pain. As I read on, I realized that it was true. My Inner Self had been there for me all along, right up to the moment in the yard when I finally surrendered to it.

At one point in Baba's book, I came across the phrase "eternal happiness." That word ***eternal*** jumped off the page at me, and my heart began to pound. I had to put the book down.

Could it be true that only the physical body dies? I thought. *That we are immortal?* I'd often heard that said in the past, but it had seemed absurd. All physical evidence had refuted the possibility of eternal anything. Now, as I considered what I'd just read, I *knew* it was true. I couldn't contain my joy! I jumped up in elation, leaping around my cell, pumping my fist in the air, and cheering ecstatically.

My mind may not have understood it all, but the rest of me did. I knew that these words were meant to be taken literally, as the absolute Truth. In that ecstatic moment, most of my fear – especially of death – vanished. *Shaktipat* and meditation had opened the door to the inner world of perfect freedom, an experience I had wanted all my life: an unbroken state of happiness and contentment.

There was nothing to fear!

And so I began a meditation practice, as Baba suggested, with great love and devotion. I sat in the same spot in the yard, at the same time of day, wearing the same clothing. No practice, no action or discipline would bear great fruit, he said, unless it was joyful, fun, and done with great respect. This was no small realization. All my life, I'd given great energy to my endeavors, but I did not necessarily feel respect or devotion. I got good results, as far as the world was concerned, but they had disastrous consequences for my life.

I had always done things because I *had* to, not because I really wanted to. I never fully embraced or gave myself completely to what I was doing. Then I'd inevitably wear myself down and make mistakes, looking forward to something else, something relaxing, or something I "really" enjoyed – anything but the task at hand. I never fully enjoyed anything or anyone; I just wanted to get things over with as quickly as possible, and so did not pay attention.

Meditation was different. I couldn't wait to get to my spot in the yard each day. Before I settled in each morning, my mind bounced from one negative thought to another – Ramona with another man, my life sentence, the scary inmates surrounding me. But a few minutes after closing my eyes, I moved deep into a state beyond thoughts, beyond pain, loneliness, and fear. My mind moved into contemplation. Within me arose quality thought, beautiful new insights and understandings. I could feel my Self move out of my body and lift high over the prison walls. I could look down at my body sitting on the ground, deep in meditation.

I discovered that the more attention and commitment I gave to my practice – to the process itself, not any desired results – the more I began to enjoy it, and the more happiness and contentment came my way. My connection to that happiness and inner freedom was so powerful that my mind and my heart seemed to be on fire every moment of the day. I wasn't focused on or interested in anything other than this incredible experience I was in the midst of.

I continued to read *Play of Consciousness*. Sometimes I would dwell on one word, one sentence, or one paragraph until I had some real insight or understanding about it. I wanted to savor the words, not move past them too fast. I never wanted it to end, so I would read as slowly as possible. And I devoted myself to my meditation practice with unshakable resolve. I meditated outside in the yard daily, without fail, no matter what the weather. I *never* missed a day, even if it rained or snowed, or if it was fifteen below zero or a hundred above.

Snow is a "security event" in a prison. When it starts to fall, the yard is cleared and inmates are ordered back to their cells. A few flakes began to float down one day as I made my way out to my meditation spot, but the "Go-Back" order had not yet come. So I sat, closed my eyes, and immediately fell into deep meditation. I was oblivious when the snowfall grew heavier and turned into a minor blizzard. After my meditation, I went back to my cell.

Later that day, the guard who usually occupied the gun tower right above my meditation spot stopped me outside the mess hall. Mr. Connors was used to seeing me out there every morning; he knew what I was doing. But that day, he told me, he'd been working the central security station, and a new guard took his place in the tower.

"So this new guy's watching you and getting more and more confused," Mr. Connors said. "After a while, you're buried under a huge mound of snow, and he can't stand it anymore. He picks up the phone and calls us in a near panic. He yells into the phone: 'There's an inmate out here, buried in the snow! He hasn't moved in an hour! I think he's dead!'"

Mr. Connors and I both chuckled. "Well, I knew it had to be you," he said. "So I said to him, 'Is this guy over by the wall at the far end of the compound?' 'Yeah!' he said. And I said, 'He's not dead, man! That's just an inmate named Gompers out there meditating!'" He laughed again.

"The best part was that very moment, when you broke through the snow and stood up! I could hear him gasp. I wish I could have seen his face. I bet he almost fell out of the gun tower. Imagine, watching you rise from the dead, shake off the snow, and just walk out of the yard!"

How can I describe what was happening to me? Until that moment of awakening in the prison yard, I felt I'd never been truly alive. Before, I'd always felt I was living in some huge dark room, an alien being abiding in a world of shadows and barely able to perceive the things around me. I never suspected that so much more existed. I accepted things as they were and struggled on with my life.

Now I had a new, extraordinary awareness, as if someone had flicked on a switch and the whole room lit up for the first time. *Shaktipat* made me come alive, filled me with awe and wonder. Everything that appeared before me was fascinating – scintillating with opportunity, pulsating with light and energy. My body was living in a maximum security prison, but my deeper reality resided in a vibrant new world. I saw everything now with fresh eyes that took in every detail, every nuance, every color and texture of the world around me.

I was intrigued by things that used to seem insignificant: the sky, the mountains, the smell of the air after a rain, the change of seasons, a blade of grass, a flower petal, ants scurrying about, a sunset, a star, even a speck of dust in the air or a piece of dirt on the ground ... When something caught my attention, everything came to a stop and I gave it my one-pointed focus. Whether I spent a second or an hour with it, I was totally present. I began to understand and learn at levels that boggled my mind. I seemed to retain everything. My memory and discrimination were clear and precise. I was operating at a level of consciousness beyond anything I'd known before, yet it was all effortless and natural.

It was as if God were taking me on a tour of the intricate beauty and wonder of His creation.

I spent the months after receiving *shaktipat* holding on tight and allowing things to happen. But I also felt I had to hold up my end by remaining aware, staying out of my head, and being disciplined in the practices. I was being turned inside out with new ideas every second of every day. I began to understand the difference between knowledge born of thinking and knowledge born of experience. My own direct experience let me know the truth and that knowledge, gathered by the intellect and experienced in the heart, became wisdom.

I saw that judging is the greatest ignorance. When I judge (or blame) someone else, I block my own heart from experiencing happiness. And of course, my happiness is never about another person, but about the way I experience my life each moment. Staying connected to my Self was not only the way to compassion; it was also the way to happiness.

Meditation allowed me to see that the intimidating ways of the inmates and guards were just expressions of their own fears and emotions, and a reflection of my own fears. Their thoughts were not connected to what was going on around them, but on what was happening inside them. And they all wanted precisely what I wanted – to be free.

When I understood this, it was easier to release my judgments and exercise more compassion. If I was impatient or angry because of someone's ignorance, I knew it was my ego popping up, that I wasn't coming from a very loving place, and it was another trap waiting to grab me. I'd suffered long enough and hard enough. There was no way I was going to allow that attitude to bring me down anymore.

I learned that the mind assumes that it is separate from everything else – but that is an illusion. This misunderstanding leads the mind into the further illusion that in order for something to happen, *it* has to make it happen. Viewing the world in this way makes it difficult, if not impossible, for the mind to trust or connect with anything outside itself. It creates our experience of separation from God, The Self, and this is always the beginning of our pain and suffering. Now I understood why I'd been so lonely and afraid all my life, and this understanding was instrumental in taking it away.

I had always needed to be in control, never realizing how exhausting it is to live that way. I learned that we live in a universe in which all that exists is one energy – God. I didn't have to do *everything* myself. I could allow myself to do my part and then relax, and trust that what I needed would be provided.

So now, when faced with a tricky, frightening, or alien situation, before taking action, I made an effort to ask *Who am I, really?* The split second it took for that question to manifest lifted me right out of my head with the awareness that I am *not* this limited self. Then, instead of reacting with my head, my conditioned thoughts, I was able to listen for guidance from within. I saw that everyone is inherently good because everyone is Divine. In judging anything, I was judging myself, because we are all One. God is present in everything and *is* everything. While I didn't always experience this teaching, I knew it was the truth.

I began to appreciate the intensity the prison setting created. It worked in perfect harmony with the *shakti* – the energy of the inner Self which was awakened through *shaktipat* – which inspired me to go inside and meditate. I could be present with people in a brand new way, without needing to be the center of attention or dominating a conversation as I used to. I could allow people to express themselves without competing with them. Filled with contentment and love, I didn't want or need anything from anyone.

As I contemplated Muktananda's teachings, I understood that if I wanted to experience the highest, I must train my mind to think the highest thoughts. I practiced turning my attention to the inner Self through meditation, and going to that place of Divine Consciousness within. Meditation strengthened my mind and gave me the ability to combat those old tendencies and thinking patterns. I began to understand how my thoughts created my moment-to-moment experience; as I became more aware of what I was thinking, I was able to change the thoughts and the experiences that resulted from them. This was an enormous revelation. Living in a state that was conscious and real, I was free to think and experience whatever I wanted. I had free will!

And when I was able to detach myself, to not identify with the mind and ultimately to allow it to become quiet, I realized directly a profound truth: When the mind is quiet, what is left is The Self, that Divine presence within me.

Meditation had unlocked an escape hatch that allowed me to dive below the turbulent waves of my thoughts to the stillness below them. But much of the time I was on the move, and not able to just sit down and close my eyes to meditate any time I felt like it. Muktananda said it wasn't necessary to close the eyes to meditate. "Open-eyed" meditation could happen continuously, no matter what was going on around us. For this he gave us a Sanskrit mantra which I understood to mean: "I honor that place of perfect freedom and joy within me which is present in all of life." He said to repeat it over and over and over again, once for each in-breath, once for each out-breath. This practice is known as *japa*, the silent repetition of God's name.

The mantra was an enormous help because it could change what I was thinking immediately. I would think the sacred syllables silently whenever negative emotions and thoughts arose, wherever I was and whatever I was doing, and my pain and fear would dissolve like magic. With the mind becoming so relaxed and calm, things happened from my heart. "When the mind is quiet, what is left is God" played over and over in me like a lullaby.

One of the many gifts meditation gave me was contemplation, the ability to stop and look deeply at something I usually would not give a second thought. Slowly but surely this began transforming my understanding of life and the people around me – even something as simple as eating lunch.

Meals in prison were handled as you might expect if you've ever watched a prison movie. Everyone in a cellblock goes to the mess hall at the same time, lines up in single file, and marches to the mess hall under guard. In the serving area you pick up a plastic tray and utensils. A dozen men wearing plastic hats and gloves stand behind a huge counter overlooking a line of open steam tables and dished chow.

In my first year in prison, I ate in the mess hall with everyone else. I was amazed and confused by how polite everyone was. As inmates approached the serving line, they went out of their way to be respectful to the servers, who were fellow inmates. It wasn't like the servers were guards, whom we were required to treat with deference.

If someone at the table wanted the salt, he wouldn't reach

into someone else's space for it. Instead, he would say, "Would you please pass me the salt?" I watched in fascination throughout meals as these hard cases practiced finishing-school manners. This curious behavior was no accident.

I tried not to attract attention to myself, but it was inevitable that I would be on the spot sooner or later. One day at lunch, an inmate asked me to pass him the salt, and anxiety reared up in me instantly. I was sure everyone picked up on it. The shaker was close to me, but not as close as I would have liked, and I had to reach a bit to get it. Feeling every eye on me, I made sure I wasn't cutting across anyone's space. I handed the salt to the inmate, and he looked me square in the eye and said, "Thank you." Relieved, I silently lowered my gaze to my plate and continued eating.

"Hey, man," he said. "I thought I said *thank you!*"

I looked up. The guy with the salt was frowning at me. Everyone froze.

"No problem," I stammered. "My pleasure, you're welcome."

His face dissolved into a beautiful, warm and friendly smile.

On my way back to my cell later that day, he caught up to me. His attitude was light and friendly, and I relaxed. He said what happened between us that morning was no big thing, and I shouldn't worry about it. "Here in the joint it's all about respect, man," he said. "You'll get the hang of it. Be cool, man." He winked at me and walked away.

As the man walked away, his words resounding inside me like a struck gong, a contemplation arose spontaneously. I had heard that word, *respect,* so much in my life: Respect for my parents. Respect for teachers. Respect for authority. Respect for God. When I did something wrong, it was because I "had no respect." When I was impatient with someone or didn't take time and care with something I was doing, it was because I didn't respect the person or the activity. I had grown to hate the word.

But now I heard it differently, the way guys doing time defined it. Here "in the joint," it wasn't so much about *respect* as it was about *dis*-respect. The essential thing was not being *dis*-respected or *dis*-respecting others. When I was focused, I was more grounded and in my heart. I was less uncertain and more aware. From that place, respect flowed very naturally, without my having to "think" about it. Respect, as I just learned, came from a much deeper place, a truer place. In order to truly respect someone else, I had to be aware and totally present with them. If I was with someone and thinking about anything else, I was ultimately disrespecting him because I wasn't paying full attention to him. I was overwhelmed by how this simple understanding could have such a profound impact on my world.

I was so in my head about not doing the wrong thing in the mess hall that I didn't hear the other inmate when he spoke to me. Respect, then, was all about being totally there, in the moment, with the other person. Taking this teaching to the highest level, I thought, respect for God was to give total attention to Him all the time. The only way to do that would be to live grounded in the heart all the time. From that place of the heart one could not help but give respect and love to both God and His creation.

Chapter 16:

Father Tom

A few months after I first read *Play of Consciousness*, I noticed another flyer on the bulletin board. It came from an ashram in South Fallsburg, about thirty minutes from the prison. It said a group of Siddha Yoga Prison Project teachers were coming to do a meditation program. Siddha Yoga: that was the name Muktananda had given to his meditation path!

I could hardly believe it! I had only just discovered this meditation path, which immediately became the most important thing in my life, and now I would have an opportunity to study with people experienced in meditation who knew Muktananda in person. I felt like a kid waiting for Christmas morning, but with a distinct edge of anxiety, partly because in prison, there's an ever-present feeling that "Christmas" may never come again.

Inmates who wanted to attend a program had to adhere to a strict security protocol. You had to submit your name and number and information about the program to the cellblock officer. The cellblock officer passed all this on to the volunteer services department to be placed on the "call-out" list. The call-out list was compiled and approved by the administration, and copies went back to the block officer and to the officers who would guard the classroom during the program. When the time came, the block officer released the prisoners with names on the call-out, and the classroom guards checked them in as they arrived. If your name didn't appear on both lists – and administrative snafus were common – you weren't allowed out of the cellblock. I knew I had to make sure to check with the block officer to be certain my name was on that list. Even then, there were no guarantees.

The night of the program finally arrived, and I was hugely relieved that the system had come through for me. The classroom guard checked off my name and waved me in. The chairs and desks were stacked at the back of the room. The floors were freshly mopped. When I saw the mantra – the same mantra I had received from Muktananda's book! – written on the blackboard in exotic-looking lettering, I got a warm feeling inside that raised goose-bumps.

Two men and two women from the ashram were already there, greeting the men as they came in. Casually dressed, friendly and down-to-earth, there was nothing unusual about how they looked or behaved, but they had a distinct quality that was different from any people I had ever met. Each one exuded strength and confidence, yet appeared open and humble. It felt good just to be in the same room with them. Three were in their mid-thirties to early forties. The fourth, Tom Toomey, was in his mid sixties. He was the one who drew my attention.

Tom, whom I came to call "Father Tom," looked like an ancient monk. He was six feet tall, strongly built and almost completely bald. His face was alive with energy and wisdom that seemed to have been gleaned from thousands of years of experience, yet there was a gentle sweetness about him. Before he said a word, his presence drew our attention. The room became still and we focused on him. I knew immediately that I was in the presence of an extraordinary being, and sensed that somehow he was going to play a significant role in my life.

That evening Tom shared the story of his remarkable life. He grew up in a large family on a farm outside Seattle. As a child, he confronted the profound questions: Who am I? What is the meaning of my life? And how can I find happiness? His search for meaning led him through careers as an engineer, a naval officer, a Catholic priest and Dominican monk, and finally a psychotherapist. Yet none of those vocations answered his questions – not even the most spiritual callings as a priest and monk.

"I thought that as a Catholic priest, as one of God's own, I would surely find what I was looking for – the true meaning of my life," he said. "But after two decades of serving God and teaching Christ's words, not only was I unable to find what I was looking for, I felt an intense need to leave the order and give up the priesthood. If I didn't leave the priesthood then, I knew I would die inside. I wasn't ready to die, so I left."

He went back to school and became a psychotherapist. It was at a psychology workshop that he first heard Swami Muktananda speak. He began to practice meditation and follow Baba's teachings. As time went on, he realized his whole life was changing for the better.

Then one day Tom had the opportunity to speak with Baba directly. He expressed his gratitude for all the blessings he'd received, and told Baba that his life was going well, but he was still unclear about what to do next. "What should I do with my life now?" he asked.

Baba looked into his eyes and said, "Do whatever you want to do. BUT: Be happy!"

Tom's story made a huge impression on me. Despite having taken sacred vows, he'd left the priesthood to follow his heart. In doing so, he had to endure tremendous pressure from his family and religious order.

As I sat listening to him speak, I could feel that same strength arising in me. I didn't have to be intimidated by anyone! I could make choices that were right for *me*. The only thing that mattered was remaining true to myself and honoring the wisdom within me. I felt freed by his experience, as if nothing could hold me back. His inner conviction left me feeling wonderfully alive.

When the program ended, I waited for everyone to leave so I could spend a moment with Tom. I wanted to express my gratitude for what he'd shared that night. But when the time came, no words would come out. I stood before him embarrassed, like a little kid. He gazed at me for a moment and then said, "Just continue to do the practices Baba has given you, and be sure to meditate every day. If you do that, everything will happen perfectly."

I left the room with his words resounding in my ears. *Just continue to do the practices and meditate every day and everything will happen perfectly.* Those words left me feeling confident and secure in my meditation practice. I floated back to my cell and fell immediately into a deep sleep.

When I awoke next morning, I felt grounded, much more connected to myself. I knew I was still feeling the power of the program, and I smiled as I remembered Tom's uplifting presence. I was filled with energy and rode it like a wave, allowing it to reveal new levels of faith and strength.

For the next month, Tom visited every week with a group from the ashram. We did *hatha yoga*, a spiritual practice that included deep breathing exercises called *pranayama* and physical postures called *asanas*, which are powerful but gentle stretches. We chanted mantras and listened to members of the group talk about their meditation experiences. And we always watched a video of Baba, whose face was magical and whose words were filled with wisdom.

I left each class feeling uplifted, excited, and clear. I felt connected to everything. I didn't have to try to *know* things: The knowledge I needed would surface without effort as a situation unfolded. My intuition became focused. I was constantly amazed at the words that seemed to fall from my lips or that took shape on a page. In my prison job as a college tutor I could answer an inmate's questions about school, then communicate deeply about personal stuff. And I never felt I was *doing* anything. All I had to do was meditate each day and stay in touch with myself. Each time I began a meditation program, I marveled at the contrast: Here I was, a prisoner, chanting and meditating in a dingy little room in a maximum-security prison with a bunch of other inmates, and feeling like I was in heaven.

The programs with Tom lasted about four weeks. After the final meeting, Tom asked to speak with me. We sat down together near the back of the room. He suggested we continue the meditation classes ourselves. The Prison Project would provide us with materials and support. Then he looked me squarely in the eye and asked if I would be the inmate coordinator for the program. I told him I wasn't qualified; I had no idea how to run a program!

"You'll do fine," Tom said. "*You* won't be running it anyway."

I stared at him, puzzled.

Tom said, "All you have to do is meditate and trust the process."

I had no idea what he meant, but I knew I trusted *him*, and I was ready to do anything to stay close to the teachings. So, feeling both uncertain and honored, I accepted.

As it turned out, Tom was right: A much greater Presence

than me was in charge of the program. I learned that the best thing I could do for others was to connect with my own heart. Grace would do the rest.

And it did: Even the guards out in the corridor were nice to us and went out of their way to help us, doing things like getting us pencils and paper or keeping the halls quiet so our meditation wouldn't be disturbed.

Some of the guards allowed us to shut off the lights for meditation. This was no small favor, as light was always a security issue and required to stay on during any program. Also, classes were required to end at a precise time so inmates could report back to the block and be in their cells for the final count of the day. But sometimes the guards would wait patiently outside the room until we were finished. It might have been only a few seconds or a minute, but it was a show of respect that we all appreciated.

The guards liked us because we were cooperative, appreciative, and respectful. We never presented them with problems; we made their jobs easy. In return they gave us as much freedom as they could. However, another reason for their kindness was the work of the *shakti*. When we left the room after each class, I could see in the eyes of the guards that they felt the power and energy of our meditation sessions. They looked as high as we did. Even inmates attending other classes on the floor quieted down when they walked near our room. The meditation energy was so powerful that it affected everyone in the building.

A benefit of becoming inmate coordinator was working

closely with Tom. His itinerary was to travel throughout the U.S. and Canada visiting prisons and doing work with the Prison Project. He would come to a prison for two or three weeks, then not return for a few months as he visited other places. Sometimes, if the program didn't catch on in a certain place, he wouldn't go back at all. I was determined not to let that happen to us. The thought of never seeing him again was unacceptable. I was determined to never let go of my connection with him, no matter what.

His letters, with their energy and love, were an important focus of my learning. His wisdom and guidance always uplifted me and helped me stay in touch with myself. As I contemplated the Siddha Yoga teachings he conveyed to me in those letters, I resolved some deep questions about my life (to say nothing about my role as inmate coordinator). It didn't matter if the specific issues that concerned me were directly mentioned or not. Everything just became clear. Along with his regular correspondence, Tom visited me on a special pass as a "pastoral counselor." Once or twice a month we would spend a whole morning diving into Baba's teachings. I treasured this time with him.

Tom was all business, a real taskmaster. I had to stay on my toes, for he wouldn't put up with nonsense for long. His only interest was his *sadhana* – his spiritual practices – and the work with the Prison Project. His life was devoted to serving God. While I knew that the core Siddha Yoga teaching was that this whole universe is nothing but God expressing

Himself in different forms, it was Tom's example that gave me a practical understanding of that teaching and showed me how to incorporate it into my life. Experiencing our true happiness – God's love – is the highest goal in every human being's life, he said. And since there wasn't anything in this universe *but* God, what was the point of focusing on anything else? Anything less than a full commitment was unacceptable in Tom's own life, and this inspired me to overcome my own distractions.

As I became more focused and committed, I also became more comfortable with his intense devotion and ways of living. It wasn't easy to stick close to Tom, because he was so independent. Sometimes I wished he'd let me rely on him more, but when he sensed I was becoming dependent, he'd pull back. "We all have to do our own journey," he would say. "Everyone has a unique path to God, and we must be true to that."

Tom was determined to help others become independent and free, never to be reliant or needy. He was always vigilant about that with me. I began to see that for most of my life I had been a dependent, insecure and needy person, and that neediness created the fears that had eaten me up inside for so long. Tom seemed to recognize that the only way I was going to free myself was to start depending on myself – and on nothing else.

This enforced independence was painful until I was able to let go of the fear. Tom sincerely wanted for me to experience the freedom and happiness he knew existed inside me. I could not manipulate him because he *needed* nothing from me, and he gave without strings. Under difficult circumstances, he would let me lean on him only until my inner connection became strong again. Then he gently withdrew, letting me swim on my own for awhile.

Over time, I realized that I could stand up on my own without leaning on anyone, and my relationship with Tom changed. It became deeper, more trusting and respectful. I could meet him unconditionally, as an equal. The stern, one-pointed taskmaster, the no-nonsense, disciplined spiritual seeker, was only one aspect of his personality. The other side, which he revealed rarely, when it was appropriate, was that of a light-hearted, sweet, comical character. He was as cute, mischievous, and fun-loving as a little boy. When he expressed that side, it was like turning on a light in a dark room, and sometimes the switch in energy was just that sudden.

One day as we sat talking about freedom, Tom brought up the experience he'd had when Baba said, "Do whatever you want to do, but be happy." Tom knew that Baba was not condoning promiscuity, which wasn't freedom at all, but utter chaos. True freedom required guiding principles and discipline, and what Baba had given Tom was the best of all guidelines: Pay attention to his inner experience of happiness. If something made him happy, if it felt truly beneficial instead of merely pleasant, he should trust and follow it. If it didn't, he needed to check his attitude toward it. If his attitude wasn't grounded in compassion for self and others, he needed to exercise discrimination and change it. He made mistakes, but he didn't see them as mistakes. He saw them as opportunities to grow.

Tom would not allow anyone to keep him from following his spiritual path, and he honored that freedom in everyone else. He was there to help people move forward with their lives, but if a person chose to revert to how he was before Tom's counseling, Tom would simply move on. He would never try to change a closed or resistant mind.

"Alan, this is the way I learn," he'd say. "This is the way I love to live my life. I will not let anyone or anything interfere with that." Tom trusted his inner guide and his sense of who he was, and he continuously reminded me of Baba's teaching that *everyone* ultimately must experience the fruits of his or her own actions.

Chapter 17:

Ohsawa

One morning after a particularly strong meditation session, I walked past the prison hospital. The front doors were being held open for an orderly who was pushing a wheelchair-bound inmate. The elderly black man slumping against the side of his chair looked frail, despondent, and utterly alone.

I felt weak and sick as the hospital odor wafted over me through the open doors. The old man disappeared inside and the doors closed, leaving me staring after someone I knew I'd never see again. And I was transported right back to childhood, a worried little boy who was terrified of getting sick and dying a painful death, like my mother.

Seeing the old man in the wheelchair switched my quiet and focused mind into one of panic all over again. I kept replaying the scene of the inmate being wheeled through those swinging doors. I kept smelling that ominous medicinal odor and feeling nauseated.

Is this some kind of payback? I thought. Is this *karma?* Am I paying for my insensitivity toward my mother at the most difficult time of her life?

And then these words rippled through my mind: *"What we think is what we become. Our thoughts create everything that happens to us. If we change our thoughts, we change our experience."* I realized my *mind* had been going off on its own, pulling me along with it.

Back in my cell, I put my headphones on and let the mantra fill me. Waves of relief spread over my body. The tension slowly dissolved, replaced by serenity. I prayed fervently for grace to reveal the insight and understanding I needed to get free of my fear of illness. This fear scared me even more than my life sentence. I drifted into a deep meditation and when I came out, I was in a different place. I was aware of a radical inner change. From that moment on I never again felt a need to smoke cigarettes or take drugs of any kind. My craving for all kinds of things fell away, never to return.

One day, two publications mysteriously appeared on my bed. One was a book titled *You are All Sanpaku* by George Ohsawa. The other was a catalog from an organic farm in Pennsylvania, Walnut Acres. To this day, I have no idea who put them there. Published in 1965, *You Are All Sanpaku* describes how modern eating habits can destroy our bodies. Ohsawa's book still lies on my bedside table; it has helped me to attain extraordinary health and well being.

Ohsawa wrote about the horrors of refined sugar, meat and

dairy products, and the poisoning of our food and drink with chemicals, pesticides, dyes, and preservatives. He lamented the voracious, unconscious consumption of food and drink that has left our culture out of touch with our bodies and our health. The result, he said, is a staggering list of diseases and a dependence on doctors, medical experts, drugs, and therapies that leave many of us powerless and frightened out of our minds. Not knowing how to take care of ourselves, is it any wonder we are afraid?

Ohsawa's words rang true to me. I decided to experiment with his recommendations. Suddenly I was sleeping deeply at night. I awoke in the morning fully rested, pulsating with energy and enthusiasm. I could not believe how much energy I had and how light and free I felt.

I began ordering from the Walnut Acres catalog and buying only organic food, mainly brown rice. Making an intention to eat organically grown foods gave me respect for my body and for my life. I now understood that my body was the temple of God. How could I possibly honor God's temple by filling it with poison and garbage? How could I avoid illness if I disrespected it in any way?

After the first few weeks of eating and living according to what Ohsawa called the "macrobiotic" way, I had more energy, stamina and focus than I'd ever had. A lifetime of maladies – allergies, joint and muscular pains, mucous in my nose and throat, energy swings, malaise – all miraculously disappeared. I began to play full-court basketball with kids half my age, never even breaking a sweat.

For the next two years, I lived almost exclusively on organic short-grain brown rice from Walnut Acres. Ohsawa praised brown rice as the perfect food: The human body can synthesize every necessary element of nutrition from brown rice. We could actually live disease-free by eating this way. And we could eat fresh, organically-grown vegetables, other whole grains and beans, and a wide variety of other foods I'd never tried. I had come to understand that the answers were within me; now I saw that this included the answers to disease. Integrating Ohsawa's teachings helped me understand the importance of dramatically changing my life. I had to eat differently, drink differently – ultimately *live* differently. Being confined in a maximum-security prison presented some interesting challenges to maintaining a holistic way of life, but it was surprisingly easy to make it happen.

We were allowed hot pots in our cells, to warm up canned food we'd bought from the commissary, but we weren't allowed to cook anything from scratch. Now, the commissary sold things like rice and dried beans, and presumably the prison administration knew we weren't eating those raw. So I just went ahead and ordered what I wanted from the catalog and cooked in my cell. No one bothered me about it.

Cooking my own meals became a treasured ritual. In my wildest dreams, I never could have imagined a day when I'd actually look forward to being locked in a prison cell listening to tapes in an ancient language, reading spiritual books and following the wisdom of an Indian guru. But now I loved coming back to my cell at the end of the day and cooking dinner, reading about meditation and yoga and reveling in the peace and contentment that arose. I cherished the hours of uninterrupted solitude.

At first the guards were baffled by the sounds coming from my cell as I chanted Sanskrit mantras, and by the scent of incense that drifted out into the cellblock halls. Certain there was something illegal about what I was doing, they'd periodically come into my cell and tear it apart, looking for something to confirm their suspicions that I was doing something illegal. That they never found anything seemed to make them more determined to catch me at some illicit activity .

One day my order of *miso* came from Walnut Acres. *Miso* is a delicious, nutritious condiment made from fermented soybeans. It's been used in Asian cuisine for centuries, and I wanted to experiment with it in my hot pot. I went to the package room to pick up my delivery. The guard saw "fermented" on the label and picked up the telephone. In seconds, I found myself being escorted back to my cell and placed in "keep-lock" (confinement twenty-three hours a day) and all privileges revoked pending an investigation.

Three days later I was escorted under guard to a hearing about my *miso*. A panel of four – two corrections officers, a lieutenant, and a civilian employee – faced me soberly from across a long table. They informed me I'd been arrested and placed in keep-lock because I was suspected of making *wine* in my cell. Although they'd found no evidence, they were convinced the *miso* they'd confiscated was contraband. That and a small quantity of raisins they'd also found in my cell were, they were certain, ingredients for processing alcohol.

I respectfully explained what *miso* was, that I used it in my food, and that the raisins came from the prison commissary. I assured them that I had no intention of making anything but soup.

The panel members asked me to wait outside. A few minutes later, a guard came and said I'd been "acquitted" of the charges, and was free to go to my regular assignment. He returned my package of miso, and after that, for several months, there were no surprise inspections. What a wonderful gift of privacy that was!

Chapter 18:

Karma

As I continued to devote myself to this miraculous path of transformation initiated by my *shaktipat* experience, I began to get deeper and deeper understanding of the form my life had taken. I began to see directly that, contrary to all appearances, I created my own experience of life. Life is actually fair.

Blame was one of the hottest topics in prison. I often overheard conversations in the prison yard, the law library, and my cellblock that revolved around the same issues: an informant had set up an inmate, an attorney had misrepresented him, a judge had been out to get him. Someone or something was always to blame.

Frankie Carbone epitomized the trap and illusion of blame. Having grown up with the mob, he was a "Wise Guy" through and through; he was the real thing, upon which the stereotype was built. Frankie was a soldier, not a boss. He was proud of who he was and what he represented and that he belonged to an elite, powerful organization. His allegiance and commitment in life were to organized crime. Everything he did or said sounded like it came from a B movie about the *cosa nostra,* or a scene out of *The Godfather*.

Frankie was serving 25-to-life for a murder he didn't commit, which he repeated like a mantra to anyone that would listen. Poor Frankie. He couldn't focus on anything else. If you stopped to say hello, within two seconds he would have launched into a tirade about how he got set up by the cops. He was convinced that he had been unfairly convicted. He was angry at the police for setting him up, at the judge for not seeing his obvious innocence, at his lawyer for being stupid and incompetent, at the DA who withheld evidence that would have proven his innocence, and on and on. He would get so worked up about the injustice of it all that it was difficult to stay around him for long.

In spite of this, everyone loved Frankie because he had a surprisingly big heart inside his tough-guy exterior. Everyone felt bad, not so much for what had happened to him, but because he suffered so much. People continuously offered advice and comfort, but to no avail. After a while there was nothing left to say. He just went on and on and you listened to him rant until you could politely get away. Anyone who saw Frankie coming ran the other way.

Never once did I hear Frankie say that he might have contributed something to getting set up for this debacle. Then, one evening in the recreation area, I overheard him talking with a bunch of his cronies about his "bum rap."

"Can you imagine?" he cried. "I must have knocked off twenty guys over the years and never got busted for any one of them. I get away with killing guys right and left, and no one can pin a damn thing on me. And then I get busted on this bullshit charge. I'm doing 25-to-life – and I'm completely innocent!"

Conversations like that made me reflect on my own case. I thought about Paul Martino, the kid who tended bar in my restaurant, who had set me up to avoid a life sentence. He received probation, I got life. How fair was that?

I thought of Steven Benson, the attorney I'd retained to defend me. He took my money, avoided my phone calls, and failed to show up in court on the day I was sentenced. Much of my loneliness and fear had been washed away by my meditation practice, but thinking of these events brought up an anger and a desire for vengeance that I never knew I had inside me. One day in meditation, I saw the sweetly smiling face of Swami Muktananda hovering in front of me. And I heard him say: "Everything that has happened to you – *everything!* – is the result of your own past actions. No *one* and no *thing* is responsible for anything that has ever happened to you. You are the *creator!* You did it all to yourself ... ***everything!***"

His face vanished and in its place appeared the faces of my attorney and the informant. As I sat looking at them, I could hear the soft echo of Muktananda's voice in the background: "... everything ... everything ..."

The anger rose in my chest. This couldn't be right! These

guys put me here – there was no question in my mind. If not for Martino and Benson, I would not be in prison. Life was unfair and unjust. They deserved my blame. I grappled with Baba's message. Then it occurred to me that my trust in his teachings was very strong, and I had nothing to lose by letting this one in. I decided to relax and listen hard to what he was trying to get me to understand.

In the next moment I had an insight so profound (and yet so simple) that it changed my life forever. I was a drug dealer! *I* was the one who sold drugs to the informant. *I* invited him to my house to buy the drugs from me. *I* made money from him. If I hadn't been selling drugs, he never would have been in my life in the first place. And while it was true that the attorney might have been incompetent, he didn't call *me* – I called *him*. It was *my* choice.

I'd been so busy blaming them for my predicament that I was blind to the truth. They had nothing to do with setting me up. *I set myself up.* Muktananda was right: I created everything that had happened. My own actions sent me to prison.

Muktananda's wisdom pierced my ignorance and resistance and revealed a new understanding. I now knew that the act of blaming was a self-perpetuating lie that locked me into an illusion that created an endless chain of suffering. There were no victims and there was no one to blame. I did it all to myself. Never again should I blame anyone for anything that had happened to me. I had to start taking responsibility for my own life. And with this, it dawned on me that I also had the power to bring to myself great happiness and freedom, simply by consciously making better choices.

I saw that thinking is a form of prayer. Whatever we think, we are asking for. And whatever we ask for, God grants. Everything we receive in this life has come to us because we have asked for it. We create our world by what we think, then we live in our own creation. Most of the time we do not see the world as it really is, but superimpose the contents of our mind on it, thinking that is reality. The problem is that we think unconsciously. We have no awareness of *what* we think about. As a result, we become confused about the source of the pleasant and not-so-pleasant things that happen to us. This was the fundamental mistake behind my blaming an outside source for my pain and suffering.

The vision of Benson's face dropped away, leaving Paul's image before me. But instead of looking cocky and heartless, he appeared frightened and lonely. I remembered how much I had liked him, how nice he'd always been to my family, especially my kids. Warm compassion arose in me. No longer did I think about what he had done to me. Instead, I was focused on his warmth and openness, his playfulness, and his struggle to find a place where he felt he belonged.

I felt as if a gigantic weight had lifted from my shoulders. I realized how much pain I had endured by holding onto my anger and my desire for vengeance. It was obvious that directing those feelings towards the two men was futile. My bitterness did nothing to them, but it was eating me up inside, and I hadn't even

known it. And now, the bitterness, the anger, the vengefulness –
were gone! In their place, these wonderful feelings of lightness,
compassion, and peace filled me completely.

Then both faces appeared again, and now they smiled
benevolently as if I'd uncovered their game and they were
relieved. On one level, the informant and the attorney had
certainly played a big role in my being sent to prison. But then
again, it was the prison experience that brought me to God. The
pain I created had brought me to my knees. When it intensified
sufficiently, and all my attempts to remove it failed, I was forced
to look within for the answers. I began to see how much I had
been given, how everything had changed for the better. There
was no doubt that I'd been set up, but not the way I'd thought
I was. It was God setting me up in a Divine process designed to
lead me to my own inner freedom. I saw that the informant and
the attorney were actually God's angels in disguise.

Finishing up my workout in the prison yard one morning, I
heard a guard bellow over the P.A. System, "Inmate #80A-2139,
Gompers. On the Visit." I had visitors.

My heart fluttered; I knew Ramona and the kids had come.
Our times together were precious. They gave me an opportunity
to share my life, as I experienced it now; we'd grown closer than
before this all happened. My relationship with Ramona was
changing dramatically. Our future together was uncertain. Yet
my respect and love for her was deeper and far more real now.

I jogged back to the main gate to receive a pass back to

my cell block. Prison regulations allowed me to shower at the block when I had a visitor; normally we could do so only on odd numbered days. I showered and put on a civilian shirt along with my prison pants. Then, full of anticipation and excitement, I went to the visiting room.

I spotted Ramona and the kids huddled in a corner at the back of the room. Adam, who saw me first, jumped to his feet and yelled "Dad!" He ran towards me, never slowing down, and barreled into me full force, almost knocking me over. He threw his arms around me and gave me what I'd describe as the perfect hug. I lifted him off the ground and saw Ramona, Alana and Jason laughing. Happiness and love shone on their smiling faces. My eyes got misty. Alana and Jason ran over to hug me. Ramona, still seated, acknowledged me with an easy, relaxed smile. I sat down opposite her and kissed her lightly on the cheek.

"I have missed you," I said. "It's good to see you."

"I missed you, too," Ramona responded sweetly.

"You know, my love," I continued, "I've had a chance to reflect on a lot of things that happened between us over the years, things I've done that were insensitive and selfish and that have hurt you deeply. I want you to know that I've come to understand things more clearly now. I realize how precious and sacred our marriage is, and that I really do love you."

Suddenly her face flushed with anger and she snapped, "Oh no you don't. You've *never* loved me."

Staggered by her intensity, I just looked at her. "How can you say that, Ramona? I have always loved you. I have always wanted to be with you and the kids. You guys are my whole life. Everything I've ever done is for you, for my family. Being with you is the most important thing in the world to me."

"That's a lie," she hissed, more enraged than I'd ever seen her. "You say you've always wanted to be with me. The real truth is that you have *never* been with me, even when you sat in the same room, talking to me and holding my hand. Your body may have been present, but your mind was always somewhere else: on your friends, your business, your precious TV sports, and God knows what else. You were never there.

"How *dare* you say you love me?"

Her words cut right through me. Ramona lapsed into silence, quivering with hurt and anger, and I watched tears fall from her eyes. The power infused in her words made me realize that what she said was true. I really hadn't been present when I was with her, unless there was something I wanted *from* her. Our relationship was centered around my own needs and desires. It was hard to face that truth, especially sitting in the visiting room of a maximum security prison, looking into the eyes of the woman I loved. Yet there it was, and it hurt so bad.

After Ramona left the visiting room that day I continued to contemplate her words: "You never loved me..." For the next several weeks, wherever I was, that scene in the visiting room replayed itself. Insights arose from a quiet, focused place within. I realized that for all the years we'd been together, my only true motivation for doing things for Ramona was to get what I thought I wanted and needed, in order to feel loved, satisfied and happy. Everything I had done was contrived, a manipulation, motivated by selfishness, insecurity and fear. I wasn't giving, I was taking. And I knew I had been operating that way all my life, getting what I needed from the world to fill my sense of emptiness and lack. It didn't matter where I got it from, just as long as I did, even at the expense of my beautiful wife and children.

I remembered how benevolent the universe was. From that understanding, I realized how I had set it all up myself. How could I have been giving Ramona real love if I was always in the process of getting what I needed for myself? Love can never be about taking, only giving. Most of the time I had been in my head, rarely grounded in my heart. I liked to tell myself that I was coming from my heart. I could delude myself into believing anything, but others knew. The universe always knew. It could be no other way.

Words of wisdom resounded inside me, like rich vibrations emanating from gongs in ancient Buddhist temples: "If you are not giving love, what is it that you are giving? If you are not giving love, what is it that you are receiving?"

To give love, I must be present. I resolved to contemplate love and my family more deeply.

Parked in the living room, right at the entrance to my bedroom in our Westchester house, was a big ugly green chair. I guess the only reason it didn't end up at the dump was because it was comfortable. But it was awkward and clumsy-looking, and never seemed to fit anywhere. At least once or twice a week I would walk by it and stub my toes on a leg that was sticking out. Hopping around in pain, I would shout, "Who put this *#!^%#$#@!* chair here?! I should have thrown this *#!^%#$#@!* thing away a long time ago! I hate this chair!" My kids would poke their heads out of their rooms and giggle at the sight of me.

One day, after whacking my toe on that chair for the hundredth time, my daughter Alana, no longer able to contain herself, walked up to me and said "Dad, you do this all the time! Why are you blaming the chair? Why don't you just look where you're going?"

Of course, her logic just infuriated me all the more. I rationalized that because I supported them and gave them nice things, they should always treat me with gratitude and respect. I expected them to be good and to do everything I asked of them.

When the kids acted out and disobeyed, or when anything around the house went wrong, I became indignant and angry. I believed my anger was justified. I saw the children as ungrateful and disrespectful. It was impossible for me to see that it was my own expectations and lack of awareness that set up these situations.

When I got angry, the children would do as I asked because they were afraid. As long as they were afraid I had some control over them. But when my back was turned, they'd revert to doing all the things I told them not to do. This would make me even angrier. The real issue was that their fear of me separated us.

They didn't do things out of respect. They did things because they were afraid.

A similar need to control governed my relationship with Ramona. In prison, before my *shaktipat* experience, I had relied heavily on her letters. They were like a drug to me. I read them over and over, poring over every possible nuance as if they were hiding secret messages. I wanted every word to be perfectly clear, totally supportive, and completely reassuring. Ramona was my lifeline, my only connection to the outside world. Without her, I felt I would be cast off, forgotten, and unloved for the rest of my life. I lived in desperation, hungry for the next "fix."

As the weeks went by, the letters began to express an ominous, disturbing energy. Something was going on that she wasn't telling me. My increasing anxiety also increased my paranoia. My mind went crazy as I thought of every horrible possibility and conjured the worst fantasies. I couldn't sleep. I couldn't eat. I constantly questioned her love for me and her fidelity to our marriage. All I could think of, night and day, was that she was being unfaithful, that I was losing her. And when she finally admitted she was having an affair, it was the single most devastating experience of my life – worse even than the day I was sentenced.

But now, after *shaktipat* and lots of meditation practice, I gained the ability to deal with these feelings, even to resolve them. I could actually face them, look them square in the eye, and then let them go. Muktananda said to let everything come that wants to come and let everything go that wants to go. He reminded us that nothing in this life belongs to us. Everything has been given to us, and in the end everything will be taken from us. Trying to hold onto things only brings pain and suffering. True contentment and happiness comes when we detach from everything. This is the path to freedom.

After a while, as I began to apply Muktananda's teaching, I was able to sit for meditation and visualize Ramona with this other guy. I would hold them in my consciousness and watch them together, allowing myself to see every possibility I could think of, everything I could imagine that normally would tear me apart. I reminded myself that Ramona had every right to live her life as she wanted. She was a free being. She belonged not to me, but only to herself and to God. If I truly loved her, as I kept telling myself I did, I would have to take a good look at what real "love" was all about.

I had always been looking for love. Since I didn't have it myself, I went out looking for it. When I saw someone who I thought could give it to me, like Ramona, I gave her all kinds of things – charge cards, clothes, jewelry, live-in housekeeper – whatever I thought she wanted. But these things were not freely offered. They always carried the expectation that she would give me back what *I* wanted: attention, sex, security, affection, children, a clean house, good cooking, and so on. When she didn't – or when anything or anyone in my life didn't give back to me after I had given to them – I felt cheated. I would become angry, frustrated, indignant, and disappointed. My whole life, until *shaktipat*, was one giant, selfish business deal.

Finally, I got it. My attempts to control and manipulate others had made them want to avoid me. Between meditation, my contemplation of Muktananda's teachings, and my own experiments in offering unconditional love, I saw that when I gave to people unconditionally, they were free to choose their own course of action. Then, since they didn't have to contend with my needs or selfish motives, they were free to focus on what mattered to them. They could make choices, if they wanted, which would allow them to pursue their own dreams. As my meditations continued to go deeper, I came to understand that real love is unconditional. Real love is an act of perfect giving. It is never judgmental. It is never a business deal or manipulation by guilt. It is absolutely free of expectation.

[Because my understanding of the nature of love had changed so dramatically, over time my relationship with Ramona grew and flourished. We were divorced after I got out of prison. She has since re-married, and yet my relationship with her now is closer than when we were married. I can genuinely say I am glad she has someone in her life who loves her and takes good care of her. There was a time when I was too selfish and insecure to do that. Again and again, my meditations reminded me to support her fully by honoring her freedom to choose whatever she felt was necessary to protect the children and move on with her life. And by letting go, by honoring her freedom, I came to discover my own. I began to understand what "surrendering to God's Will" meant. I simply offered my love, then got out of the way.]

The *shakti* continuously pushed me to resolve issues with my past. My contemplations showed me that I could never resolve things *for* other people. My only responsibility was to give my heart to others, to share my feelings unconditionally and without expectations. The *shakti* was showing me how a real relationship worked. While in the outside world, I never would have bothered to consider how my actions affected other people. But now I was drawn to reflect and meditate. I spent hours contemplating the way I'd led my life. I saw how selfish and insensitive I'd been and how I'd disappointed many who loved and trusted me.

I also realized that I'd never *wanted* to hurt anyone, which brought me comfort and self-forgiveness. I wanted everyone to know how much I'd learned about myself, that I wasn't the same person anymore. I wanted to share these feelings with everyone from my past, especially those whom I felt I'd hurt, to let them know how truly sorry I was. I wanted to help them out of their own negative feelings in some way.

When I sat down with pen in hand, I would begin to write without thinking, spontaneously letting go. Whatever needed to come out, did. I could feel my energy build until I was ecstatic, yet I stayed centered. It actually grounded me so firmly that I felt I could do anything. I was free of thoughts and all distractions. I wrote and wrote, sharing my experiences, insights and new understandings. My heart felt clean and my intentions pure. I knew I couldn't change anyone, but I could change myself through this action. When I left my expectations out of it and just offered it all to God, I was okay with whatever response came back, whether forgiveness or anger.

Almost everyone I wrote to answered to say how profoundly touched and inspired they were by what I said and how much it helped them to work through some of their own limitations and problems. Most of those relationships dated back to the Mark Serrano era, in my stock market days. My Aunt Mary, who was my godmother and who once loved me, lost money when her stocks went down and never forgave me. I wrote her but she never replied. I wrote to Jack Banning, with whom I was in business when I was arrested. Of course, our business had collapsed. I wrote extensively to my daughter Alana. I wrote to Ramona. And I wrote to my brother.

My relationship with Lou was badly in need of healing. We'd always been extremely competitive, fighting over the most insignificant things. When we argued, we each took a position that rationalized everything from our respective points of view, so we always ended up in a stalemate followed by long silences. I self-righteously blamed my brother for creating the problems between us, and he blamed me, leaving us both angry and alienated.

Lou had a way of issuing injunctions when he got worked up. Being forbidden to do something by my older brother really pushed my buttons. As I got older and more comfortable with myself, I learned to back away from the intensity and the controversy, but there were times that months, even years, went by without us speaking to each other.

Things had come to a head during my time as a stockbroker. When the firm collapsed and the DA began his investigation, my clients were asked for information in the case against me. When I discovered that my brother had been called in, I was furious, certain that he had betrayed me. It never occurred to me that I was the one responsible. Our relationship was strained from the day the company went bust, and by 1975, we stopped talking entirely. When I was sentenced, it had been nearly five years since we had spoken a word to each other.

I finally realized that as long as I was locked into believing I was right, there was little chance of resolving things between us. I wrote him a letter that spoke my heart. I didn't ask him to forgive me. I didn't ask him to visit me. I simply said that I loved and missed him, had thought a great deal about what had happened, and realized that I'd hurt a lot of people. I could not change what I had done, but I wanted him to know that I was committed to using this time to change myself.

The following week, to my surprise, my brother Lou and sister-in-law Trudy came to visit me at Eastern.

In a county jail, visitors usually communicate with prisoners through a Plexiglas partition, talking into telephone receivers. In a maximum-security prison, the overall security precautions are much tighter, so ironically you actually have more space and freedom than in a lower-security lock-up. The visiting rooms at Eastern were large and fairly comfortable. There were vending machines for soda, coffee, cigarettes, candy, and sandwiches There was even a big mural painted on one wall depicting a beautiful green mountain with a waterfall. You could use it as a background for family snapshots that were so natural-looking, you'd hardly guess they were taken in a maximum-security prison.

There were chairs and tables scattered around the room where inmates would play cards, do paperwork, or read to their kids. There were also private rooms with glass partitions where inmates could meet with their lawyers or even be interviewed by the media. *Good Morning America, 60 Minutes*, and other news programs had interviewed some of our more infamous inmates in those rooms.

When you have a visitor, a guard comes to your cell to let you out. If you aren't in your cell, they announce your name and number over the loudspeaker in the yard. If you are anywhere else, your name appears on an "out count" that states your location so you can easily be found. You are then given a pass to take a shower and change into a street shirt to wear with clean prison pants.

I was always excited to have visitors, of course. I loved to go to the visiting room. It was an opportunity to stay centered and meet friends and acquaintances as the person I was now. It was challenging, especially with those who had known me for a while, because they expected to see the person I used to be. My challenge was not to get caught up in anyone's expectations. My visitors felt uncomfortable at first because they assumed I was the old me. But they usually left with a new, positive perspective about me and, in most cases, our relationship was transformed.

Trudy and Lou had visited me once before, at the Westchester County Jail right after I was sentenced. Because we hadn't been on speaking terms, they had had no idea that I had been in any kind of trouble. They were stunned and frightened and didn't know what to think. On this visit, they arrived with their hearts in their hands and tears in their eyes. We stood together in the middle of the room in a three-way embrace. When I finally looked up, everyone in the visiting room was looking at us, nodding and smiling.

I felt the years of separation and anger melt away. There was no way to deny the love between us. All the years of arguing and competing, all the resentment and anger that had separated two brothers for so long, dissolved the instant they walked in. There was no longer any need to compete. It all seemed so stupid now. In fact, nothing from the past mattered. I was simply happy and grateful to be with my brother again.

Every time Trudy tried to talk, she would break down crying, but talked through her tears. My brother looked more lost and afraid than I had ever seen him. To begin with, he was uncomfortable being in a maximum-security prison. His take on prison was based on what he'd gotten from newspapers, movies, and television. He believed my life was in danger and had no idea what it was like for me. They repeatedly said, "Oh, Alan, we have to get you out of here. Are you all right? Are they hurting you? Are you frightened? Are you lonely?" Their only agenda was to get me out. We were a unified, dedicated family again and it felt wonderful. My drug bust had brought my brother back into my life and allowed my sister-in-law to love me openly.

Shortly after that first visit, Lou and Trudy began looking for a second home. Although Lou lived and worked in Pennsylvania, almost three hours from the prison, he bought a house not thirty minutes away. He claimed that he didn't buy it because of me, but that he'd always been looking for that kind of house. But deep down I knew otherwise. From then on, he visited me almost every weekend. He brought food, clothing, books, and many things that made my life easier. When I became a vegetarian, they began bringing me food. We were allowed about twenty-five pounds of food from the outside each month. Right on the road outside the prison was a little vegetable stand that a local farmer set up to sell organic vegetables and fruits. Whenever Lou and Trudy visited me, they stopped at that stand. My brother also would leave money in my account so I could order things from Walnut Acres Farm. They took extraordinary care of me, and I know it made them feel good. It was healing for all of us.

On many visits they brought my nephews, Michael and Geoffrey, who were seventeen and twenty-two. Today they are both lawyers, Michael with the Legal Aid Society and Geoffrey with a successful private practice in Philadelphia.

Until everyone felt more comfortable being in the prison environment, we mostly discussed my situation. But after a few visits I talked to them about my meditation practice, my spiritual initiation, and all the profound experiences and changes going on in my life. They were fascinated, especially Michael, the youngest. To this day he still meditates and follows a macrobiotic lifestyle.

In time, I came to realize that all the years spent battling my brother, trying to outdo him and show him up, were an attempt to gain his love. I hadn't understood that I could never *get* love from him, or anyone else. It was only when I found love inside myself that I was able to give it. The moment I realized that, I knew what real love was. I also understood that it didn't matter what anyone did with it, only that I intended to give it unconditionally, without motive or expectations. And that's what I have done ever since.

Chapter 19:

Lifers

You cannot truly know anyone else until you know yourself. As my understanding of my own life continued to deepen, so did my understanding and compassion for those around me. I saw with different eyes now. I found the inmates fascinating. Everyone seemed to have a unique mystique. I was making a very real connection with this remarkable community, and I felt deep affection for each and every one of its members. I began to see my fellow inmates with genuine love and respect, while seeing how they, too, were creating their own worlds. It was an amazing experience.

Prisoners are constantly involved in manipulation – of family, girlfriends, other inmates, the administration – anyone who might have something they want. What they wanted revolved around four general themes: homosexual activity, drugs, special privileges, and getting over on other inmates or even their wives, girlfriends and families. To "get over" on someone is to take

194 ❖ Maximum Security

advantage of him for one's own gain. For example, someone might tell another inmate, if you do this or that for me, I'll pay you back with a pack of cigarettes when I next go to commissary. Then when commissary time comes around, he swears he never made that promise. If the inmate accepts that story without retaliation, the other inmate has "gotten over" on him.

Many prisoners were emotionally insecure with low self-esteem. They needed agreement from others and they needed to demonstrate their power. They used the intensity of these needs to manipulate a situation or to take control of a relationship. This is how they got what they wanted. But more important, "running a game" on others, and succeeding at it, made them feel important and powerful and gave them a temporary sense of self worth.

Hanging around these guys, of course, could put you between a rock and a hard place. If you were unsure of yourself, you'd be open to manipulation and end up doing something out of fear of the consequences of not going along. And sooner or later one of these "favors" would get you thrown into "the box" (solitary confinement) or even charged with a new crime and sentenced to more jail time.

Inmates occasionally asked me to do something because they thought I was easy. They didn't know about my "secret weapon" of silence. It is extremely difficult to manipulate someone who doesn't speak. To get a person to act, you first have to get them to say something. The game keeps going only as long as there is some verbal exchange, for without it, the manipulator is just talking to himself.

From that place of silence I could see right through the game. I didn't have to do anything. I would just listen, looking directly at the speaker, sometimes for long stretches of time – ten, fifteen minutes or longer – without saying a word or shifting my focus while they spoke. I discovered that being silent, yet attentive and always respectful disarms the other person. He eventually would grow impatient and frustrated and give up, or would feel heard, and walk away satisfied. Either way I stayed out of trouble, often made friends, and learned a great deal about others and myself.

One example of this is an incident in which I was asked to toe a racial line – and didn't. I had become friends with Edmond, a deeply religious black man. Being new to the world of spirituality, I enjoyed walking the yard, listening to him share his spiritual experiences. One day after one of our walks, Santo, a white guy from my cellblock, caught up with me. He was a real street character, and heavily connected to organized crime. I'd noticed him watching Edmond and me; the longer we talked, the more agitated he seemed to become.

Santo began by acting friendly, like he was about to do me a huge favor by steering me in the right direction. "We have a lot of 'good people' (meaning other organized crime characters) living in the same cell block with us," he said, "and they would not think very highly of a person like yourself hanging out with no black guys. It would also give the other guys in our block a bad image of us, especially if we was to be seen with you doing this. And that would not be a good thing."

Translation: He liked me a lot but didn't feel he could continue to be seen around me if I were going to continue to hang out with black inmates. In the past, a speech like that, with its violent undertones, would have intimidated me. The guy was obviously trying to scare me and get me to do something for him.

I got real quiet and listened carefully. I began to see that, as tough as he tried to come across, he was frightened in his own skin. I started to feel bad for him, and immediately realized I didn't have to do anything he proposed. I merely listened, which seemed to make him feel good, that I was giving him respect. When he finished I thanked him politely and headed back to the block.

I continued to walk with Edmond after that encounter, without hesitation or fear, and more important, without defiance or arrogance. I simply chose to do what I wanted with my time and my life. No one ever spoke to me about it again, and, amazingly, Santo changed his demeanor toward me. We became very good friends. He even started coming to the meditation classes, and little by little began to take steps toward his own personal freedom. (We are still friends today, some twenty-six years later, and it is a friendship that I value with my whole heart.)

When I first arrived at prison in the summer of 1980, I lived in fear of provoking an attack by some inmate by saying the wrong thing, and therefore, adopted silence as a defense. I withdrew from any interaction with anyone. That ploy did keep me out of trouble, but did nothing to ease my fear.

After my first meditation out in the yard, silence took on a whole new meaning. My fear was gone, as was my self-consciousness about being silent. I could be quiet and observe life unfolding within me and around me. I could monitor my inner state, noticing when I was beginning to feel intimidated or self-conscious. Maintaining silence helped me to quiet my mind and stay detached from disturbing thoughts, and the challenges of prison life.

Through silence, I eventually became able to be present with everyone in a way I never could before. I no longer felt the need to be the center of attention, or to dominate a conversation. I was able to let people express themselves without competing with them. I was amazed at how much I enjoyed simply listening, really hearing what was being said. I was more patient and loving than I'd ever been before. Most important, I didn't want or need anything from anyone. I was so filled with contentment and love that I didn't have to go outside myself to get it. This certainly was no overnight transformation. At first, a mere word or thought could break my peace, the way a pebble creates ripples on a calm lake.

One morning I was in the corridor on the way to my cellblock, feeling deeply calm and secure. I spotted a guy everyone called "The Greek." Instantly, I was anxious and fearful. Meditation had allowed me to let go of most of my fear of the inmates, but the energy around The Greek was a different matter. He gave off a sinister vibe that bordered on evil. The sight of him made my skin crawl. But as I walked by him, I became aware of my great companion and refuge: Silence. I didn't have to speak. I didn't have to try and figure out what to "do." I simply went inside myself, like a turtle pulling his head into his shell, and kept walking.

As I passed, I overheard The Greek "talking trash" about me to another inmate, words clearly meant for my ears. His intention was to provoke me and thereby justify a reason to come after me. Making eye contact would have been enough.

I listened to the guidance emanating from the stillness within me. Everything began to happen in slow motion; I could see where to place my feet, how to carry myself, even how to breathe, without creating tension or drawing attention to myself. I felt myself relax and get centered again. A moment later The Greek disappeared from sight.

I marveled at how little it took to disrupt my equanimity. None of this was about The Greek or what he could do to me. It was all about me. When I forgot to attend to my inner state and allowed myself to become frightened, I unconsciously shifted my focus from my heart to my head, shutting down my confidence. "Unconscious" is the key here. Pain and suffering result from *unconscious* actions. An enlightened being – a free and happy being – would never choose pain and suffering because he is conscious of his actions and his choices. So when I *consciously* remembered the Self, the silence of my heart, I reconnected with the power of my true state.

This gift required moment-to-moment alertness, a continuous invocation of awareness. Forgetting my true Self was a deeply engrained old habit for me, and I needed to stay vigilant. Now I was choosing to remember, to be aware, and then to act on that awareness. There was quite a steep learning curve to this practice. Sometimes I would "wake up" for a moment and realize that I'd been doing things without having any awareness that I'd been doing them. And most of the time, I couldn't even remember what I had done that day or five minutes before. It was an incredible insight for me because it got me to see and understand the prodigious distracting power of the mind, and how much of my life was spent in unconscious thinking and actions.

This process of waking up, again and again and again, became a vital part of my spiritual practice; I began to view it as nothing less than the path to liberation.

Occasionally I had to break my silence and actually decline a request. I was used to spending evenings in my cell, reading Baba's books, listening to chanting tapes, or writing. I was very content; the solitude and peace made this time important to me. Every night as my door slammed shut, instead of feeling anxious and lonely, I was content and secure.

But one night, just for a change of pace, I took one of my favorite Siddha Yoga books and ventured down to the cellblock "rec" area. Every other night after chow, we had the option of going down to the recreation area in the basement from 7:00 to 9:00.

The rec room was a fairly large area that could hold about a hundred people. The walls and floors were concrete, which the inmates had covered with a thick coat of glossy gray paint. Chess and checker boards were set on wooden picnic tables, there was a Ping-Pong table, a TV area in a corner with wooden benches to sit on, and picnic tables where inmates could play cards or talk. There were also a few old dusty mats you could exercise on, but no comfortable couches or chairs. Everything was made of very hard wood and after awhile your butt let you know it was alive and well.

Thirty or forty inmates came down each night. The atmosphere was fairly reserved, not the way it was at Riker's Island or the county jail. Inmates doing "big time," especially in the maximum-security prisons, were usually more mature, respectful and less rowdy than the short-timers in the less-secure facilities.

I sat at an empty table, took out my book, and began to read. A few minutes later, an inmate from my cellblock came and sat across from me. Now, this was no ordinary inmate. This guy was one of the most unpredictable, notorious, and dangerous inmates in the entire prison system. He'd spent more than twenty years incarcerated, mostly in juvenile detention or state-run mental institutions, and he was not yet forty.

John Iglesias was his full name, but everyone called him John-John. The prison system was full of guys like John-John. He had been into drugs most of his life, which ensured a life of prison time and emotional suffering. He was about six feet tall, with dirty blonde hair, blue eyes and a fair complexion. He would have been really good-looking if not for two things: the paranoia in his eyes and the speed at which he moved, spoke, and thought.

Physical exercise was one of the few things that slowed him down and calmed his mind. He worked out all the time, running around the track in the yard, lifting weights, or doing endless pushups and sit-ups. He also played on the prison football team and pitched for the softball team. He was a different person after running five or ten miles, and right after he worked out it usually felt safe to be around him.

When John-John was at his most dangerous and unpredictable, there was something wild and paranoid in his eyes. That look was my signal to be somewhere else. But when he was relaxed and present, he was fun to be with and real friendly. However, even in those moments, I remained aware of the constant possibility that he could swing the other way in a flash and lose control. When he did, he was capable of anything. In fact, he was the one responsible for the bloody mess in the corridor that Bigfoot was cleaning up the night I arrived at Eastern. John-John had fractured the skull of another inmate with a lead pipe.

There he sat, staring across the table at me with his mad, paranoid gaze. I sat very still, wondering what he could possibly want from me.

"What is that you do out in the yard every day?" he asked. "Meditation? What's that about?"

I was surprised. He was clearly on edge, eyes wild. Meditation was the last topic I expected him to bring up.

I answered slowly and carefully, not very grounded in that moment. I was in my head and I was afraid. But as I spoke, I began to realize that he really wanted me to talk more about meditation. My fear eased. John-John seemed to relax a bit too. The wild look in his eyes slowly disappeared, and he became almost shy. We spent the next two hours talking about my meditation experiences. He seemed fascinated and moved by what I told him, at least when no one else was within earshot. But if someone came by, he became self-conscious and uncomfortable.

Just before go-back, another inmate approached and whispered something in his ear. When John-John turned toward me again, his calm had vanished and the crazed look was back. He pushed something at me under the table. I glanced down; it was a paper bag. He told me to take it back to the cellblock with me.

John-John was constantly looking to get over, and he was usually successful. He could be charming and persuasive in a boyish, innocent way, but underneath his words there was a dangerous vibe. I knew the bag contained drugs. If I did what he wanted and got caught, I'd jeopardize any chance of ever getting out of prison again. Even if I did what he wanted and didn't get caught, I would become known as an easy touch, and in prison that was not the way I wanted to be perceived. But if I refused, I would have to contend with him every day from then on.

I froze. I could neither move nor speak. My mind raced, searching desperately for some way out. My initial reaction was to just take the bag. *You won't get caught*, my mind whispered.

Who would ever suspect you of doing something like this? Just take the bag now, and you won't have to deal with John-John later.

And then another part of me spoke up. *Don't do it! Are you crazy? You will be putting the rest of your life in jeopardy.*

Suddenly, from a place deep inside, I felt strength and power build. It was like a dam bursting. It filled me completely, charging up through my chest to my neck. When it reached my head, my mouth opened and I said, "I can't do that."

I was shocked. It was hard to believe I'd just faced this guy and denied him. Even more amazing was the perfect delivery of my confident and fearless response. For some time I remained focused on him, almost hypnotized by the insane look in his eyes. Finally he stood and slowly came around the table to where I sat. My heart thundered; fear charged back up inside me as he closed the short distance. And then it subsided as I felt, once again, the warm surge of strength and confidence. I was no longer afraid. I sensed at the root of my being that I was being protected. I knew everything was being handled by the *shakti*, and that I didn't have to do a thing.

John-John was now practically on top of me. He sat down. His eyes had softened once again, and his demeanor relaxed. A tiny smile quivered at the corner of his mouth. He reached out and put his arm around my shoulder and looked straight into my eyes. "Man, you're outta sight," he said. He gave my shoulder a final, friendly squeeze and got up and walked away.

When I got back to my cell, I tried to make some sense out of the scene. I could not have responded more perfectly if I'd rehearsed for a hundred years. Face-to-face with an individual more dangerous than anyone I'd ever encountered in my life, and on the verge of doing something so risky and irresponsible that I would have compromised my freedom, I had responded with more courage and conviction than I ever knew I possessed.

I discovered in prison that unconditional acceptance is what real friendship is about. It was a great teaching, not to try to change anyone, to enjoy people wherever they are at, to accept them totally and never judge them. Perhaps one of the unlikeliest friendships I developed was with Harry, the guy cleaning up the blood in my cellblock the night I arrived. The other inmates called him "Bigfoot" because he resembled the mythic missing link of the North Country. Close to 7 feet tall, Harry weighed every bit of 350 pounds, and had not shaved or cut his hair since he'd arrived at Eastern fourteen years before.

Harry was serving two consecutive 25-to-life sentences for slashing two men to death (nearly decapitating one of them) in a bar fight. He never spoke much about his case. I learned most of the details from other inmates. The story was that he killed the men during an LSD blackout. He had gone wild, pulled out a huge hunting knife, and took on everyone in the place. No one believed Harry would ever see the outside world again. He stayed in his cell almost all the time, which he refused to clean in defiance of prison regulations. His cell was right next to mine and we talked together quite a bit. Sometimes we talked in the corridor on cleaning days when the cells were unlocked, or now and then in the yard when Harry decided to venture out of his cell. The best times were after we were locked in for the night. We could talk through our windows as we looked out at the magnificent sky. It was peaceful at that time of night, especially with the serene mountains to gaze at.

Over time, Harry shared some of his life with me. He told me he used to get high on acid all the time. He said he did so much acid that after awhile the only way he could get high was to "mainline" (shoot it into his veins). After several years, he started blacking out when he wasn't high. He hinted that when he had a blackout, he was capable of anything. He never remembered hurting anyone, but found out about what he'd done from witnesses afterward.

Harry thought that his drugging had shifted something in his brain so that now, without taking anything, he could be propelled spontaneously and without warning into altered states of consciousness. He confided that that was why he stayed in his cell most of the time and rarely went into the population. I was not comforted to hear this, but it got me into the habit of being aware of his eyes. They always let me know if he was present or not. After I got to know him pretty well, my sense was that he was probably better off in prison than out in the world.

I loved the moments with Harry when he was lucid, and full of wisdom and light. They were deep, lasting and important, and they set the tone for a relationship that I sensed was different from the ones he had with his other friends. I felt great affection for Harry, although it was not something I expressed outwardly. I believe my conversations with him about meditation, supported by the quiet energy that meditation had given me, had a strong effect on him. He eventually asked me if he could borrow some of my books, especially the ones by Muktananda. Harry was a prolific reader who had been reading about Eastern philosophy for years. He had a brilliant mind, and often read two or three books in a day. Unfortunately he rarely let anything in. He was self-protective and didn't trust easily. To say he was paranoid would be an understatement. I needed to respect his space and not try to sell meditation to him.

Harry was intuitive and immediately picked up on where people and situations were at. For that reason, very few people, guards included, ever tried to get over or play games with him. He commanded respect from everyone, guards and inmates, mostly generated by his overwhelming size and mien. Everyone stayed clear of him, even the guards, but they decided to make him cellblock porter so that he could be out of his cell when everyone else was locked in. Once people got to know him, they respected him because of who he was and how he carried himself. Harry said his grandmother was a wealthy baroness in Estonia before the Russian Communists confiscated the land and riches of the wealthy families. Before fleeing the country for the United States, she managed to bury her money and jewels. She drew a map to the treasure – a map that Harry still had. One day he showed it to me. He said the treasure, worth millions of dollars, was still there.

"I'll probably never get out of prison," he said. "But you will.

If you go after it, I'll share it fifty-fifty with you."

"Isn't it dangerous to go into Estonia?" I asked.

"Well, it's still under Communist control," he said. "I guess it could get a little tricky if you were caught."

I chuckled. At that point in my life, money was the last thing I was interested in. My wealth was in my spiritual path and in the riches I was given through meditation. I looked at Harry respectfully and said, "No thank you, my friend. That's not where my head is at anymore, but I hope you find someone willing to take it on."

He tried once or twice more to talk me into finding his grandmother's buried treasure, but eventually gave up.

Every time the *shakti* made its presence known, something profound changed inside me. I no longer felt intimidated by The Greek, John-John, or Harry. I had gained their respect. Even more amazing was that the general intimidation I'd grappled with for so long seemed to have dissolved. I was comfortable walking around the prison complex. I felt that I fit in, that I belonged. In place of insecurity and fear, I felt a confidence that covered me like a protective shield. I was no longer concerned about other inmates or what they thought of me. And yet the next deep inner experience would push me from this safe, protected inner space into a new, more involved position in the prison community.

The night after the *miso* hearing, I picked up one of

Muktananda's books and became immersed in it. As I read, a strong energy began to fill me. (This kind of thing happened to me often after *shaktipat.*)

On that night, like the other times, the energy was inspiring and exciting. My awareness became intensely clear and very focused. Thoughts vanished. Background noises faded away. There was consciousness, a sense of being aware, but not of thinking about anything.

When I first read Muktananda's words, I intuited that they were important; they resonated so powerfully. But I was not clear about the meaning of a lot of it. That night, as I was reading, everything became magically clear and his teachings and words came alive. I understood what he was saying at a far deeper level. The sudden insight kindled a hunger to express it in words.

The next thing I knew, I'd picked up a pen and was writing feverishly. Words and ideas flowed effortlessly. A simple idea became a philosophical dissertation, as I filled page after page. I was aware as I wrote that my mind had become still, focused on the ceaseless flow of energy gushing up from within. Later, when I read back what I'd written, it was like seeing those words for the first time.

When I first received *shaktipat,* experiences happened within, as a complete inner shift. There wasn't very much focus on the outer world or other people. All my meditation and contemplation made me feel incredibly full. I had made an authentic connection to my Inner Self. That night after the *miso* hearing, I sensed I was more grounded in my heart than I'd ever been, and that it was time to come out a bit more and share it.

A balance was needed as an outflow of what had filled me. To fully embrace the oneness of the universe, I had to include the rest of God's creation. So the *shakti*, in her divine wisdom, began to send me back outside.

Chapter 20:

Mujahid

Next day, as I made my way around the prison, many inmates seemed interested in talking with me. Talking had always been a way for me to hide from others, as well as from myself. Silence had changed that. It made me a better listener – if I didn't think I had to say the right thing, I could stop reacting, slow down and relax. Now, in that relaxed state, with the inner connection meditation had given me, and with a state that was more and more defined by love and compassion, words came.

I began to look for situations where I could share some of the experiences, wisdom and insight I was receiving. I was like a plug looking for a socket. People responded – inmates, guards and many of those on the prison staff.

Sometimes it started with a nod of the head, a smile, or a simple "how you doin'?" Then came the small talk, the going-nowhere conversation. But we invariably moved to deeper, more personal issues. A deep sense of trust developed with some of the guys out of those conversations, and that in turn gave me confidence to speak from my heart. In the midst of a conversation, I had little awareness of much more than the joy of flowing with the exchange. But at a pause, or at the end of a conversation, I was exhilarated, and usually that exhilaration was shared by both of us. The other person's body language and facial expressions would change from cool and low-key to animated, expressive and openly happy. Sometimes it got so high that it ended in a spontaneous hug of happiness. Guys would say things like, "You're all right, man," or, "Thanks, for that, man," or simply: "I never looked at it that way. Thanks a lot, man."

I talked about concepts that worked for me, especially *karma* and blaming, which always seem to be at the root of my spiritual understanding and are so often the keys to releasing the blocks that create pain and suffering. And while talking about them repeatedly may have helped *others*, these exchanges never failed to deepen *my* understanding. I discovered that giving in this way, without being preachy or imposing, was an act of love. It was uplifting both for the other person and for myself. It clarified many of the teachings and insights I had been given. It solidified my own understanding at the same time that the other person moved to a new place.

The power of living from my heart allowed me to tune in to the other men. The issues were similar: were their wives or girlfriends being faithful, would they make parole, would they get new trials, when would they get out of prison? I concentrated on the issues as symptoms of the real cause of tension – The Mind – and this opened up the possibility of talking about meditation, although I usually didn't use the word until we had established some understanding and trust.

We talked about how it feels when the mind is too active and how it feels when it is relaxed and peaceful. We talked about how our whole experience of life changes when we are not identified with and lost in our thoughts.

For many of these guys, this was another world. The *concept* of peace certainly wasn't foreign, but the *experience* of the concept was. They were under tremendous pressure and tension, and so of course they continuously looked for peace. But their search always ended with drugs, alcohol, tobacco, sex, material success – anything to kill the symptom, and nothing that would address the cause.

I had learned through meditation and Baba's teachings that overcoming pain and suffering begins and ends with the mind, with thought itself. The quieter the mind, the more peace. No thoughts? No pain! The moment they saw this possibility, they could experience it for themselves. The idea that real peace was an "inside job," not something that resulted from external circumstances, became real to them.

But the most popular topic by far was freedom. Prisoners are obsessed with freedom. They assume that when they leave prison – when they are "free" again – they'll be happy and suffer no more loneliness and tension. When I asked if they were happy before they lost their "freedom," when they were still out in the world, they admitted they were not. They acknowledged that they'd landed in prison because their lives didn't work when they were on the outside and "free." When a prisoner began to accept that freedom did not lie on the other side of the prison walls, his mind stopped for a moment. And then we'd begin to talk about *real* freedom.

One day not long after I became coordinator of the meditation program, one of the Muslim inmates told me that the *imam* – their religious leader, and a fellow inmate – wanted to speak with me at the prison mosque. The imam was Mujahid Abdul Halim, who, as Thomas Hagan, was serving 20-to-life as one of three men convicted in the 1966 assassination of Malcolm X. Next day, I went over to have an afternoon chat with him. My tranquility was a tribute to the power of meditation; I felt no anxiety or intimidation. As I headed over to see him I repeated *We are all the same being.* That teaching let me meet Mujahid as an equal.

At the entrance to the mosque stood a burly Muslim inmate dressed in white. He escorted me inside where several inmates were lighting incense and candles, moving chairs around, sweeping the floors. They were immediately aware of me – a white man, and a Jew besides. The energy they put out wasn't exactly negative, but it was definitely strong.

Entering the mosque, I was enveloped in tranquility and in a familiar meditative energy. It was a big room with rugs on the walls, sweet incense, and pictures of Muslim spiritual leaders.

Most of the inmates in the mosque wore traditional Muslim robes, a beaded necklace and a *kufi,* a skullcap similar to the Jewish *yarmalke,* but broader and more colorful. The center of the room, used for prayer and meditation, was empty.

Wearing a green kufi and a white robe, Mujahid was seated in a chair at the front of the room. There was something regal about him – not quite the portrait of the violent assassin I'd expected. He was about six feet tall, strongly built, stocky, maybe 200 or 210 pounds. I was used to seeing him in his prison uniform, so his green robe gave him a strikingly different persona.

He motioned for me to come forward and I was escorted to a chair next to his. The other inmates stopped what they were doing and sat down to listen. Right away I could see that my calm, confident state allowed him to relax. Mujahid spoke deliberately, measuring each word. His face was expressionless as he looked at me, but his eyes radiated tremendous energy. He began by asking about the meditation program I was facilitating, saying he'd heard good things about it. I assured him that I had very little to do with it, that it was the power of the meditation itself that ran the program. All I did was work at staying connected to the energy and letting it guide me. I said the program was open to everyone, regardless of religion or belief system. Meditation was a divine and universal gift that everyone could benefit from. I then extended an invitation to him and all the brothers at the mosque to come and check it out.

Mujahid nodded politely, then motioned one of his followers to escort me out of the mosque.

Maybe he was just being polite. But I was glad that I'd had the chance to meet him. The very next day, he sent three of his followers to meditate with us. Over the next few weeks, more Muslims came to join us, although Mujahid himself never came. I'd heard rumors that the Muslims disliked and distrusted white people, but I never felt even the slightest evidence of this. Clearly, their presence was Mujahid's endorsement of the program and an expression of his trust in me. The Muslims who attended enhanced the powerful energy already present.

As time went by, Mujahid would nod or say hello as we passed each other. Sometimes we'd exchange a few words. He was interested in talking about meditation, and thanked me for the positive changes he saw in those followers who were meditating with us. I always felt uplifted after talking with him, and appreciated that a personal trust had developed between us. Wherever he appeared I watched him. Usually a number of Muslim brothers walked along with him, as humbly as disciples. Mujahid was always expressionless, dignified, and detached. He did not seem like an inmate, but an exalted leader who was given tremendous respect by inmates, prison officials and guards alike.

The administration recognized his influence over the whole inmate population, and at times called on him to intervene in potentially volatile situations. I witnessed one of these interventions one Saturday afternoon in the winter of 1981. Most of the population had gathered in the auditorium for the weekly movie. Everyone had saved the snacks they'd purchased in the commissary, and sat there crunching away. I always found it amazing how often one of the inmates sitting next to me would offer me some of his food. Most of the time, it was someone I hardly knew. The feeling here was far nicer than it was on movie night at Sing Sing. However, on this day at Eastern, the atmosphere was electric, filled with tension. Angry and frustrated, the inmates were agitating for better treatment. They had made their grievances known; they wanted more privileges, better food, and more effective communication with the administration.

There was talk of violence, even a riot, if things didn't change. In the midst of all the commotion, a deputy superintendent arrogantly walked out on stage and motioned for everyone to quiet down. Instantly the crowd started to yell and stamp. The superintendent's arrogance turned to helpless bewilderment as he waited for the noise to die down. Finally realizing that wouldn't happen, he stalked off the stage to the cheers of the audience. The inmates yelled for the movie to begin.

In the midst of the deafening chaos, I noticed something happening at the front of the auditorium. Mujahid walked onto center stage. He stood there motionless and the racket slowly subsided to utter silence. Everyone, white and black, focused on this man, waiting for him to speak. Finally, Mujahid raised his head slightly and spoke with great eloquence and power. In just a few moments his powerful charisma commanded everyone's attention including that of the guards and administration. When he finished, he nodded respectfully to us and walked quietly off the stage. There was no applause, just complete silence. The issue was resolved. Mujahid had defused the situation.

Having become friendly with some of the guys on my cellblock, I began looking forward to going to the rec area. There was a group from Colombia whom I especially liked. Like me, they were not typical jailhouse guys – they had tasted the good life. Most of them were well-educated, intelligent, and from wealthy backgrounds. Being in prison was hard time for them.

Their families lived far away and rarely, if ever, visited them. Their marriages and relationships were often doomed by their long prison terms, which were generally life sentences for drug running. Because of the animosity of the U.S. toward Colombia, it wasn't likely that they could look forward to a new trial or a reduced sentence. Just being a Colombian national in the U.S. was tantamount to waving a sign saying, "We are drug dealers!"

These guys were frustrated and angry because if the police suspected that a Colombian might be involved in drugs, or even lived in an area where drug trafficking was going on, he got busted. Then it was up to him to prove his innocence. The way they saw it, the US Constitutional guarantee of presumed innocence didn't apply to Colombians. The drug laws were harsh at that time, with a 92 percent conviction rate. Many Colombians were afraid to stand trial. Rather than chance a 25-to-life sentence if convicted, they pleaded guilty to a lesser charge, even if they were innocent. They were profoundly distrustful of our government, the police, and most of the people they came into contact with. They stayed together as a group and talked only amongst themselves.

Although inmates avoided the Colombians, I enjoyed hanging out with them. They helped me learn Spanish and I worked with them on their English. In that exchange a sense of trust developed between us, and they began to confide in me. Over many months, we spent many nights talking about the pain and fear so many of them had kept locked inside. As we talked, they began to see and accept the karmic circumstances they had created. They gradually lightened up and released some of their frustration and pain.

My relationship with the Colombians taught me about the real meaning of trust and its impact on our ability to live freely and joyfully. I saw how much those frightened, contracted men suffered because of their distrust of everyone around them, which effectively incarcerated them within their own minds. The moment they were able to trust just a little bit, their hearts opened and they were able to breathe the breath of freedom once again.

Chapter 21:

Jason's Miracle

One day, a guard opened my cell door and stuck his head inside, "Gompers, your counselor wants to see you."

Every inmate is assigned a counselor whose job is to maintain a personal relationship with the inmates in his care. Ideally, the counselor helps inmates adjust to prison life, acts as a sounding board for frustrations and problems, and, when necessary, as an intermediary between inmates, the administration, and family. In reality, however, the counselor is a watchdog, a pair of eyes to monitor the emotional and psychological attitudes of the inmates in his caseload. In this way, the administration can be made aware when someone might present a problem to himself or the prison population.

Initially, I saw my counselor, Dennis Bligen, about once a month, but after the first few visits, I only saw him three or four times a year. At first Dennis asked the usual, by-the-book

220 ✤ Maximum Security

questions: "How are you doing? Is everything going all right for you? Are you experiencing any problems? Are other inmates bothering you, intimidating you, trying to get over on you?"

After a while, I realized that he was a really decent guy and I began sharing my meditation experiences with him. He was amazed by some of the things I told him, more astounded and moved, by how happy and content I was. Our conversations began to revolve around meditation and the teachings of Muktananda. Ultimately we got to really like and respect each other, and a relationship developed that transcended my days in prison. I met up with him about a year after my release when I applied to teach meditation as a prison volunteer at Greenhaven Correctional Facility, where he was the acting superintendent.

But on that day at Eastern, I had no idea why Dennis was calling for me. I wasn't concerned. In fact, I was happy for the opportunity to see him again. Dennis looked up and smiled as I entered his office. He motioned for me to sit opposite him, and folded his hands before him.

"Your wife just called," he said. "She wants to speak to you. I think there was an accident of some kind at home, but I'm not sure. She was so upset on the phone that I couldn't quite make out what she was saying." He handed me the phone.

As I dialed Ramona's number, I felt a deep, tranquil state arise within me. I heard a voice within say, *Stay detached but be sensitive. Come from your heart. Everything is fine. Don't worry, no matter what you hear.*

Ramona picked up after one ring. I said hello, and she fell

apart. She was hysterical, totally out of control. I knew that any attempt to talk to her at that moment would be futile, so I stayed still, listening to her, allowing her to express the emotion and pain.

"My baby, my baby," she wailed. "Don't let him die. Please, God, don't let him die!" She couldn't stop. She continued crying and ranting hysterically for several minutes more until she finally quieted down, eventually to an almost imperceptible whisper. There was a pause and she asked, like a little child, "Are you there, Alan?"

"I'm right here, my sweetheart," I said. "Tell me what happened."

"Jason was hit by a car. He's in the hospital, in intensive care. He's in a coma and we don't know if he's going to live or not." Again she broke down sobbing. "It's not fair! He's so young! I love him so much! Why don't they take me instead?"

As I listened to Ramona, a powerful conviction arose within me – *Jason would recover, he was all right!* I waited calmly until she regained her composure again. "Don't worry, honey," I said. "Jason's all right. Don't ask me how I know, I just know. Jason is not going to die, I promise you."

I asked her to hold on while I talked with my counselor. I explained the situation to Dennis, and he said he would try to arrange an emergency clearance to visit my son. I relayed this news to Ramona.

"Please come soon," she whispered in a half-sob.

"Nothing bad will happen," I said. "Jason has so much love around him. He's protected. You can trust what I'm saying. I know it's true."

In times past, I would have gotten angry and frustrated because I couldn't personally respond to the situation. I would have automatically assumed that it was my responsibility to make things right, to rescue my son and save the day. I would have gotten myself crazy with anxiety and tension, and blamed everything and everyone for my predicament. But this time I was calm and steady, ready to act on whatever insights came to me.

Early next morning, I was taken to the front gate of the prison and briefed by the two corrections officers who would drive me to Beth Israel Hospital in the city. As they snapped on handcuffs and shackled my feet, they warned me that any attempt to escape would be handled with absolute finality. I said I understood, my only intention was to be with my son, and they would have no problem with me.

As we drove along I felt an intense anxiety rising within me. I began fervently repeating the mantra, and as the miles rolled by, my state changed. The mountains were magical, beautiful. I hadn't seen the outside world for over two years. I gazed as though I were seeing it for the first time. A warm energy inside me permeated my entire being. At times it felt as if the car would just lift off and fly away.

I repeated the mantra for the entire two-hour trip to New York. By the time we arrived, I was in an incredible state –

wonderfully light and detached and thoroughly confident that Jason was going to be all right.

One of the guards opened the back door and removed the shackles from my feet. He said he would take the handcuffs off in the elevator, even though he wasn't supposed to. He winked at me, and the message was clear: He trusted me. His simple act of kindness touched me deeply. I no longer saw him as a guard. Any separation between us had vanished.

We entered a huge elevator and, as promised, my handcuffs were removed. It felt wonderful to free my hands and get the circulation going again. Stepping out of the elevator, I found myself face to face with my whole family. My eleven-year-old daughter, Alana, ran over in tears and hugged me. Nine-year-old Adam, who was absolutely adorable, was right behind her, but he was so shy that he couldn't look at me.

As I stood talking with Alana, Ramona spotted me and began to cry. I quickly made my way to her. I put my arms around her tenderly and pulled her very close to me. She said Jason was still comatose. Though his vital signs were good, each day he remained unconscious made complete recovery a little less likely.

"I'm going in to see him now," I whispered. "Don't worry. Everything is fine. I'll be back soon." I kissed her, then entered the intensive care unit.

A nurse said I could only have a minute or two with him, and showed me to his bed.

Except for all the tubes attached to him, he looked like he was just sleeping. For a full minute I gazed at his angelic face. Suddenly I felt my heart burst and my whole body fill with love. I was unable to move. I could feel a current of love pouring out of me and into my son. I moved closer and whispered, "Hi, J, it's Dad, can you hear me? I'm here. You're my best guy. I love you. Open your eyes, sweetheart, I want to look at you." His eyelids fluttered, slowly opened, and then he was looking right into my eyes. We remained locked into each other's gaze for a few moments, then he whispered ever so softly, "Hi, Dad." Then he closed his eyes and drifted off again.

A warm and beautiful wave of relief, then certainty, filled my being. Jason would make it. Of this I was absolutely certain.

Muktananda says we should take refuge in the mantra; it protects those who repeat it. On the long drive to the hospital that day, down through the peaceful mountains, the mantra had quieted my mind and put me in touch with the *shakti*, God's power inside me, so when I saw my son I was filled with love instead of fear.

I stood up straight. My eyes were wet and I was totally drained. I took a deep breath, then walked out into the waiting room. In the midst of a goodbye hug, Alana looked up at me. "Daddy, why did this happen to Jason?" she asked. "Why do *you* think it happened?" I replied.

She took a moment, her little brow furrowed in thought, then said, "You know, Daddy, Jason always drifts off a lot," she said. "I never know where his head is at most of the time." She paused a beat, then looked up at me again and said, "Maybe this was God's way of waking him up."

Later that day Jason came out of the coma. The next day he was out of intensive care. Four days later he was home. I was told that the hospital staff thought his recovery was a miracle.

Chapter 22:

Clemency

The first thing Lou and Trudy did after I went to prison was to work on getting me out. Lou suggested filing an appeal and getting a new trial. But an appeal would mean hiring a lawyer and spending a lot of money, and I no longer had any money. When Ramona sold the house in Westchester, she offered to put half the money in a bank account for me for when I got out. I told her to keep it for herself and the kids. My faith was huge. I could feel grace supporting me. This situation had its destiny and purpose. Everything would work out and *was* working out, every moment.

I didn't want my brother to spend his money on me, either. Besides, I sensed that an appeal and a new trial were unlikely. Grace got me into this predicament and when the time was right, grace would get me out. This faith was neither blind nor intellectual, but based on an inner experience that I could feel in my bones.

But my brother insisted. He was so sincere that I finally decided to let him help me. I also recognized the need to be proactive when opportunities arose, when the *shakti* offered them. Real success, I understood, involved actions undertaken with awareness, consciousness, and discrimination.

So my brother had his part in the play and was acting out of love, purpose and focus. When I surrendered to his participation, it felt perfect. Whether I got an appeal really didn't matter to me. What did matter was the fact that we were a family again, working together with love.

Lou got the trial transcript and began interviewing renowned and successful attorneys who specialized in appeals. He found two or three who agreed to read the transcript and offer an opinion about my chances for an appeal. Each of them independently concluded that we had no chance at all. In fact, one attorney said that it seemed as if my attorney had deliberately closed the door to an appeal by failing to raise any objections at the appropriate moments at the trial.

Another attorney cited an option we could explore. He asked to visit me and talk about it. That excited my brother, whose hopes were raised instantly. My immediate impression of this lawyer was that he was very honest and had great integrity, but he also couldn't find anything in the transcripts that could have been used on appeal. He was interested in my case mainly because of what he called the "horrible sentence" that had been imposed for the relatively small amount of drugs involved. But he could find no issues that might be appealed.

I asked about the issue of "ineffective counsel." The attorney said we could make an appeal based on that issue, but it was a long shot at best because the appellate courts were inundated with such appeals. He said he would handle it for us if we wanted to go that way, but it would be expensive and our chances of winning were slim. "But," he said, "there is a reasonable chance of getting Alan executive clemency based on three key facts: The case had involved only an ounce and a half of cocaine; the trial judge had said, on the record, that he would not have given Alan that sentence if the law gave him discretion; and the New York state legislature was considering changing the Rockefeller drug laws, under which Alan had been sentenced."

The lawyer said we needed to collect letters of reference from friends, family, former bosses, teachers – anyone who was willing to stand up for me. More importantly, we needed letters from senators, congressmen, judges, prison personnel. In the meantime, Stan said he would draft the petition. My brother footed the legal bills and he and Trudy went after collecting letters for the file. They assumed this huge undertaking with great enthusiasm and devotion.

One day in 1981, just before Thanksgiving, I was doing laundry in the cellblock when the PA system squawked, as if clearing its throat, and issued the order: "80A-2139. Gompers. Report to the security office." I had no idea why the security office wanted to see me, but I'd been here long enough to know that calls like these rarely meant good news. A guard handed me a pass and said the warden wanted to see me.

It was a bit of a walk to Warden Phillip Coombe's office. I had plenty of time to get worked up: *Why did he want to see me? Did I do something wrong? What is going to happen?* But no – I didn't allow myself to go there. My mind was calm. I was not upset, but curious, looking forward to meeting the guy. I marveled that I wasn't experiencing any concern. In the past, a call like that would have sent me into crisis mode. I'd never spoken to Warden Coombe, a hands-on kind of guy, a sort of a George Steinbrenner of the prison system. He was always trying to improve things, and was considered a role model for other wardens in the system.

He would walk around the yard and the halls greeting inmates by name and stopping to chat, and he took their complaints seriously. They trusted him. He was the kind of guy you knew in high school as a strong teacher – you didn't mess around in his class. He was starchy, meticulous, fair but serious-minded, and he didn't smile much. In fact, he never showed much of any emotion, so when I turned the corner and saw him standing outside his office, I blinked in surprise.

This was not the cool, reserved Superintendent Coombe I expected. He looked almost anxious, pacing a little, sort of wringing his hands. When he caught sight of me his face lit up, and he rushed over, grinning. He grabbed my hand, pumped my arm, and threw his other arm around me.

"Mr. Gompers, I am so glad to see you today!" he said. "Please come into my office and make yourself comfortable."

Warden Coombe's office was roomy but not huge, nicely furnished in a civil-service kind of way. The carpet was an inoffensive gray. The wall behind the large wooden desk held commendations and photographs of the Warden shaking hands with various functionaries and politicians. He waved me into a brown leather couch that dominated another wall and dragged over a straight-back chair for himself.

Coombe shut the door, sat down, and leaned toward me, elbows on knees and fingers steepled. "Mr. Gompers, do you have any idea how many inmates there are in the New York State prison system?" I shook my head. "There are over forty thousand men and women incarcerated in New York State prisons," he said. "Each year, the governor grants executive clemency to a handful of those inmates. This year he has chosen five." After a dramatic pause, he added, "And *you* are one of them!" He sat back, beaming.

For the next minute or two, we just sat there staring at each other, as Superintendent Coombe anxiously awaited my response. I wasn't being indifferent or insensitive. I simply didn't need good news anymore to lift my spirits; my spirits were already "up." I was content with and committed to my spiritual path and ready to go wherever it led me. I wasn't looking for anything or even thinking about when or if I was going to get out of prison. I smiled, thanked him for all he'd done for me, stood to leave, and shook his hand. He handed me an envelope and wished me good luck. As I walked out of his office, I could feel his eyes on my back. I turned to wave, and chuckled inwardly at the puzzled look on his face.

But on the way back to my cell, a wave of intense anxiety caught me by surprise, stopping me dead in my tracks. There was a knot in my stomach that I hadn't felt since my *shaktipat* experience in the yard a year and a half ago. I stood there in the corridor and tried to figure it out. The slight weight of the envelope in my hand drew my attention; was that what this was about? For all I knew, its contents would send me back out into the world the next day. I had no money, no job, no home, and no wife. I thought about it a little longer, then had a startling realization: *I didn't want to leave.*

I wanted more time. All my life I'd thought of time as the enemy. It represented the thing I feared most: death. But now I valued time as a priceless gift more precious than anything the material world could ever give me. My time in prison no longer felt like a sentence. Prison had become a sanctuary, an opportunity to find true freedom. It had become my home, not a home of concrete and steel, but an inner home that I could take with me wherever I went. It wasn't the physical prison itself that I wanted, but rather the time and solitude it provided.

Outside prison, I had lived with fear and an addictive need for the twin security blankets of success and approval. In this maximum security facility, I indeed had found maximum security, the true meaning of freedom, the unassailable security that only freedom can bring. I longed for more time, time to continue going deeper in my meditation practice, time that would allow me to become so grounded in my true Self that no one in the world, no event in the world, could shake my inner freedom ever again. What better place to continue this search than in prison, where I first encountered this true freedom?

Back in my cell, I tore open the envelope and read the letter. The governor had reduced my sentence by nine years, from 15-to-life to 6-to-life. I sighed in relief; I still had four and a half years. With the letter still in my hands, I gazed out the window at the soft green mountains beyond. Time seemed to stop and I drifted into a state of complete serenity and contentment.

It's not about getting out, whispered the inner voice that had become my unfailing companion. *It's about getting free, and you're not there yet. You're here because this is the ideal place for you. Here - behind these walls - you can hear Me.*

From that moment, life in prison blossomed even more. I began to revel in every moment more fully than ever before. Even the most insignificant little object seemed to explode with fascination and wonder for me. I had a clear feeling of having nothing to "do," and a total absence of anxiety and expectation about anything. My life felt complete, at least with respect to everything that concerned my past, and my future was focused on being right here, right now, in the present moment. And it felt wonderful.

All the skeletons were out of the closet. There was nothing more left from my past that could surface and come back to haunt me. Of course, I knew more was yet to come, but I was no longer concerned. I was "awake" and alive to myself, and through *shaktipat* and my new consciousness I was fully armed for what I needed to do and how to work with things when they did happen. This made all the difference in the world. I didn't want anything, need anything or look forward to anything. I was exactly where I needed and wanted to be.

Chapter 23:

Work Release

In the winter of 1985, my counselor Dennis told me that because of my exceptional record in prison, despite the fact that I was a Lifer, I had an excellent chance of getting into a work release program. I'd be eligible to apply in a few months. He'd be happy to add his personal recommendation to my application. If I were accepted into the program, I'd be transferred to a work release facility where I'd be allowed to leave each morning to seek employment. I would have to return each night, but could spend weekends with my family.

Work release! It would mean I'd be reunited with my children and my friends. I would meet the world head-on again, this time armed with new conviction and strength. I was ready.

Dennis forwarded my application and scheduled me to appear before the work release panel, which operated like the parole board. On the appointed day, I formed an intention to stay focused on the yogic principle of detachment. By now I has learned that expectations were the primary cause of our frustrations and disappointments, so I needed to let go of expectations about the outcome.

When my name was called, I paused before entering the hearing room. I vowed to stay connected with the energy of my heart, to stay focused and relaxed. If I were granted work release, great. If I were denied, that would be just fine, too. The steadiness of my state was far more important to me than the decision of the panel. This intense real-life situation was a perfect way to put my meditation practice to the test. I took a deep breath, gave myself permission to relax, surrendered to the power of the *shakti* within, and opened the door.

The room was bare except for a long table and six chairs for the panel members on the other side, and one chair for me facing them. It was designed to be intimidating, but I have always loved an audience. I felt an electric sense of challenge go through me, the same way I responded to every situation when I was on a stage to perform. In that moment, I felt totally present, in *the zone*, and my attention was aligned with the process and not at all with the outcome.

They were a motley crew, a mix of men and women between forty and sixty years old. I scanned them searching for a friendly face, a warm smile, a look of compassion – someone, something to connect with. Nothing. Their energy was cold and distant. In addition, most of them looked unhealthy and out of shape. *The inmates in prison with me look much better than they do*, I thought. *How ironic!*

I would have to rely totally on myself, and not depend on anyone for help. I went straight to the mantra and I was back to myself. The questions began:

Mr. Gompers, how do you feel about being labeled by society a drug dealer and a felon?

I said I fully recognized that I was a drug dealer. If I had been the person back then that I was now, I would never have sold drugs. But the truth was that when I did, I was not aware of how much I was hurting other people, especially my family. I would like to change what I did, but I can't. What I can do is live in the highest way possible from now on.

Mr. Gompers, was society justified in having done this to you?

Yes. I was a drug dealer. This being so, I acknowledged that society not only had the right, but the responsibility to look at me from that perspective. I accept this totally.

How can you ever feel good about yourself again knowing the kind of person you are and all the people you have hurt?

I told them I'd learned to meditate while serving my sentence and that this practice had transformed my life. Meditation gave me an experience of my Inner Self, my soul. It showed me that there is good in everyone, including myself. I had never experienced anything like that before. I'd always felt unworthy, unloved and lonely. I have an anchor now, a foundation.

Through meditation I have become aware of an inner happiness and contentment that I never knew was there. It has put me in touch with the person I always wanted to be and never knew how to find. I am happier now and more at peace with myself than ever before. I know I cannot change what I have done, but I know that I am not the same person that I was, the one who hurt so many people. I cannot convince anyone of this. Only the way I lead my life from now on can demonstrate that.

Mr. Gompers, do you still use drugs?

I said no; meditation gets me to a far better place than drugs ever did.

You are not a very nice person, are you, Mr. Gompers?

I agreed that, for most of my life, I wasn't a very good person, although I always wanted desperately to be one. I now know, deep inside, that I am a good person. I have stopped measuring that person by what he has done in the past; that is no longer who he is. I have discovered that I am much greater than that. That other part of my life is over.

What kind of father can you ever hope to be?

A better father than I have ever been, I said. Since I've been in prison, my wife has managed to bring the children to see me regularly. Although they are still very young, I feel that they've noticed the change in me and we have grown closer. Of all the things in my life that have haunted me, my past neglect and insensitivity toward my children hurts me the most. I have no way of knowing when or if I will have another chance to be with them again. But right now, each time they visit, I make the most of that time. No matter what happens, I know how much I love them, and I can feel their love. For me, this is the essence of being a father, and I am grateful for whatever opportunity I get to give them my love.

Why should this panel let a person like you back into society again?

I said that I hoped they'd seen inside me enough to know that I spoke from my heart and from my Truth. Then they would know that what I said was real.

By the end of the ten-minute hearing, I noticed that the energy in the room had clearly shifted. At no time in front of the board did I ever become angry or intimidated. I continued to repeat the mantra and offer my love, respect and blessings to the panel, no matter what happened or what they said to me. As I stood to leave, one of the men on the panel, who'd been particularly strong with me, came over and introduced himself. He smiled warmly, shook my hand, and wished me well. The others still wore their game faces and conservatively wished me luck. Though I didn't want to have any expectations about the outcome, I felt very good about the way the meeting went.

Several days later Dennis told me I'd been approved for work release.

I had been at Eastern for five years. I was 44 years old. So much had happened, so many changes, transformations that had forever altered my life. In the past, dealing with change of any kind was so hard that I'd fight to hang onto whatever felt safe, even life in a maximum-security prison. Now I could see clearly that it was time to move on. It would be a huge transition. I was excited and felt certain that only great things were waiting for me out there.

But leaving the prison that day was quite emotional. Saying goodbye to so many people, guards as well as inmates, was far more difficult than I imagined. There was so much love expressed that I found it hard to keep my composure.

An inmate from my cellblock, a young Chinese guy named Chin, stopped by my cell to give me a painting he'd made for me. It was hard to imagine how such a gifted thirty-year-old could have been in prison since he was fifteen. The painting became a cherished memento, and a powerful reminder of all that I had been given during this time.

Harry, my outrageous and wonderful next-door cellmate, also came by to say farewell. He looked into my eyes and reached out to hug me – all seven feet of him. He actually lifted me off the ground. I realized how much I loved him and would miss him. He appeared calm and grounded, but sad. I sensed that his heart was heavy even though he tried his best to hide it.

[Shortly after I left, I heard that after fourteen years, the prison administration had finally ordered Harry to clean his cell, cut his hair and shave his beard. He had refused on all counts and barricaded himself in his cell. The riot squad was sent in and beat him so badly that he spent almost six months in the hospital, but not before he did some major damage to a half-dozen guards. From the hospital, he was sent to solitary confinement, then shipped out to another prison farther upstate near the Canadian border. When I heard the news it broke my heart. It seemed as if Harry had given up on his life. I have heard nothing of him since.]

I was supposed to be sent to a work release facility (a halfway house) in the Bronx called Fulton. Instead, for some undisclosed reason, seven other guys and I were sent to Fishkill Correctional Facility, a medium-security prison about an hour from New York City.

Initially, we were told that it would be just a few days before we were go to a work release facility, but we were warehoused there for almost four months. We were housed under guard in a trailer outside the barbwire fence, and were escorted from the trailer to the prison mess hall three times a day. The rest of the day we were confined to the trailer. Three evenings a week we were allowed into the prison for recreation time.

No one seemed to know what to do with us. We weren't part of the prison population, nor were we free to come and go. We couldn't take advantage of the work release program because Fishkill wasn't set up as a work release facility. We existed in a state of limbo, doing odd jobs, reading, playing cards, or watching TV. In the early 1900's, Fishkill was a prison for the criminally insane. An elaborate underground tunnel system had been constructed to move prisoners from building to building. It looked like a set from a horror movie. My first journey through the tunnels was more confusing than frightening. It was dark, wet, and eerie, and the air reeked of a rancid odor almost like decaying flesh. A corrections officer was posted every twenty-five yards or so, so it felt safe enough to keep moving along, until after about a hundred yards, I came to a fork in the tunnel.

The tunnel to the right was known as "No Man's Land." Although it was a shortcut to the main part of the prison, few inmates ever took that route. It was dark, there were no guards, and the inmates believed it was haunted. It led to an old hospital complex, where lobotomies and other medical atrocities were supposedly performed on inmates around the turn of the century.

I gazed into the dark reaches of No Man's Land. *I'm in no hurry*, I thought. *No need for a shortcut*, and took the tunnel to the left.

But later that night, something from one of Muktananda's books grabbed my attention – something about fear being the final barrier to total freedom. In order to be totally free we have to face every fear, in every situation, and move beyond it.

As I read his words, the darkness of No Man's Land leaped into my mind, along with a realization: *I chose not to take the shortcut because I was afraid.* No, my mind objected. There was simply no logical sense to go into that area, it rationalized. But I knew the truth.

I wrestled with this insight throughout the night. When I got up the next morning, I was resolved. This situation was a blessing and had been given, as all things are, as an opportunity. I knew there wasn't any real danger in that tunnel. The superstition and fantasy scared everyone. It wasn't the old hospital that frightened me, but the *thought* about it that triggered a fear that *already* existed in me.

I felt that I'd understood what I was meant to understand: not to walk into a dangerous situation just to prove that I was man or that I was brave, but rather to bring to an end the mental construct, the illusion created by my mind, that there was anything to fear. That evening, on my way back from recreation, I decided to face my fear head-on and take the short cut through No Man's Land.

As I approached the fork in the tunnel, a wave of anxiety arose. I stopped, gathered myself, drew my *mala* (prayer beads) from my pocket, took a few deep breaths, and walked into the darkness. With rapt concentration, I took refuge in the mantra, knowing it would protect me. I moved forward into the shadows, my heart pounding.

Within minutes I felt I'd penetrated an uncharted world. There was almost no light. The only sound was an occasional echoing *plop,* as a drop of water from the ceiling fell into a puddle below. I was totally alone. I repeated the mantra more vigorously with each step. Gradually, I began to make out the outline of the entrance to the old hospital just ahead. As I reached the doors and was just about to sigh in relief, the energy in the tunnel suddenly changed.

It seemed as if the walls of the building began to pulsate, as if they had suddenly come to life. Every inanimate object around me appeared to be aware of my presence, and the walls began to close in on me.

They were right! My mind screamed at me. *It is haunted!* I thought I could hear the wails and cries of long-dead inmates being tortured by sadistic, cold-blooded doctors performing hideous acts on them.

Somehow I had the presence of mind not to allow myself to be swallowed up by this madness. I looked down at my mala beads, solid and heavy in my hand. The minute I recognized that I was still repeating the mantra, a wave of relief and comfort flooded through my whole being. I felt absolutely protected. The tension lifted, and with it, the fear.

After that night, I made it my business to take that same route at every opportunity. In fact it became a ritual. Each time, I would concentrate intensely as I walked through No Man's Land, striving to see it simply as pure energy appearing in the form of the old hospital complex. The journey became easier and less scary each time I made it. Within a week I could walk through it as comfortably as I did out in the sunlight.

It was clear now that there is an essential difference between real danger and the illusion of danger created by a thought. What one needs is the wisdom to know the difference. And for this I felt enormous gratitude.

Chapter 24:

Going Home

Finally, finally I was put on a bus and sent down to New York, to the Bronx, back to my roots. But my excitement wasn't merely about returning to my old stomping grounds. It was more about the surprising new appreciation I had for this most amazing place. Before prison, I had come to feel lost and lonely in the vast city, disconnected from everything. But those feelings were gone now, replaced by a deep longing to once again embrace the excitement and energy of New York. I had no job, no real place to go and no idea what the future held, but I was happy and confident. I was going home!

Fulton Correctional Facility was a halfway house set up for inmates on work release. Rather than throwing us back out into the world without money or means of support after one to twenty-five years behind bars, the system gave those of us who qualified a year to work out the transition.

It is a wonderful and compassionate idea, I thought, as the bus headed down the mountainside toward New York. *It makes so much sense.*

Fulton was an old apartment building in a run-down neighborhood in the middle of the Bronx, opposite Crotona Park, which separated the East Bronx from the West. Everything was set up barracks-style, an arrangement I hadn't had to deal with during my years at Eastern. My mind was a bit agitated initially, but I repeated the mantra, got myself centered, and set an intention to use the situation as another opportunity to practice detachment.

My dorm housed about twenty-five guys, most of them under thirty. Unlike the maximum security atmosphere I was used to, everything was disorganized, loud and chaotic. All the lower bunks were taken, so I wound up with an upper one. It felt strange to sit on my bed and look down on everything, but I was determined not to allow anything to affect my state. Being in the world again would be quite a challenge.

We were assigned counselors and had to complete an interview process before we could leave the facility and look for work. This process took almost a month, during which time we filled out psychological questionnaires and met with our counselors for brief sessions. I was finally approved for release and given a date to begin my job search. My counselor required me to submit an action plan, so I circled some listings in the Help Wanted section of the classifieds for jobs as a salesman, and as a waiter. Although everything happening was new to me,

I wasn't experiencing any fears and concerns. I had no idea what I wanted to do or where I would wind up, but I had complete faith in my inner guide. I relaxed and trusted that everything would work out perfectly. I was beginning a new life; I was on a great adventure.

On the morning of my release, I met with my counselor to receive her final instructions and get my pass. She told me to be back no later than 3:00 pm that afternoon, and to keep a written record of who I met with and what transpired in any of my job interviews. A long line of inmates was already waiting when I arrived at the release center at 8:00 am At the front of the line two correction officers sat behind a big desk. I took my place at the end of the line and soon found myself becoming agitated. I was anxious to get out into the world again. It seemed this would take some time, and I wanted the line to move more quickly. *It's a normal reaction*, I told myself, but I was not comfortable. So I closed my eyes, took deep breaths and allowed myself to slow down. As my whole being relaxed and became clear, I asked, *What's the message for me in this situation? What do I need to learn?* The answer came instantly: Patience!

Let the game come to you, a voice deep inside reminded me. *You are an eternal being. What's the rush? Where are you going? Enjoy the play!*

With that insight, the edginess and tension began to dissolve and I was able to let go.

Right in front of me in line was a Spanish kid in his mid-twenties who was animated and excited. He was from my dorm; we hadn't spoken before, but we acknowledged each other. He told me he'd been "down" (in prison) for eight years and hadn't seen the street since he was seventeen. His whole family was waiting for him outside the facility, including his girlfriend, whom he was planning to marry as soon as he was paroled.

He kept saying how happy he was and how much he had to look forward to. He was through messing around with drugs and hanging out on the streets. God had given him a second chance and he was going to run with it and do the right thing. His mood was infectious. It took us almost half an hour to get to the head of the line. When his turn came, the young man shook my hand. "Well, wish me luck, here I go!" he said, his face wreathed in an enormous smile.

As I let go of his hand, he turned quickly to face the desk and the guard behind it.

"Wipe that smile off your face you punk-ass mother f***er, and pay attention to what I'm goin' to tell you," the guard bellowed.

In an instant, the beautiful, engaging smile on the young man's face turned into an ugly scowl. The transformation was so dramatic, it seemed as if a different person had taken his place. For a split second, I thought he would leap over the desk and go for the guard's throat, but instead he began a barrage of expletives that brought the room to total silence.

The guard pointed his finger in the kid's face and warned him that he was treading on dangerous ground. But the kid was out of control and each time the guard warned him to calm down, he became more furious and irrational. Within seconds, a half-dozen correction officers appeared and grabbed him from behind. But nothing could stop him. He continued to scream obscenities at the guard behind the desk. He fought like a wild animal, the veins in his neck distending as if they'd explode.

Then the guards had him in handcuffs and, in a flash, he was gone. I stood there staring at the door he'd just passed through. In one surreal moment this young man had destroyed his life and dreams. A few minutes before, he was happy, excited and filled with possibility. In the blink of an eye, it was all gone. I was trying to gather a perspective on what I had just witnessed when I heard the same officer shouting obscenities again. This time he directed the tirade at me. I had my back to his desk and was apparently holding up the line. I quickly turned to face him.

I did not react to anything he said. I stood silently before him, waiting for him to finish yelling at me. He carried on a while longer and then stopped and glared at me through narrowed eyes, daring me to say something. He was taunting me as he had the Spanish guy. But I was not walking into that trap. All my years of meditation and all of Muktananda's teachings, in that moment, were there fully to guide and support me.

This was *the* moment of yoga. *This* was where the practices become practical, where theory becomes reality. I could allow this prison guard to break me down and cause me to lose my contentment and power, or I could stay grounded and focused in my heart, no matter what he did. I understood that he could lock me up, or let me go on my way. He had that choice and the power to back it up. But *I* had a choice, too, and *I* had power: I could choose to accept whatever happened, and I had the power to do that without losing my contentment and inner freedom. This is the ultimate choice, and it is the only one that mattered.

As I was reminded of this great teaching, every part of me came alive and gained strength. It didn't matter what he did to me. I didn't need anything from him or from the world. What I wanted was to stay connected to who I was, and to maintain complete faith and trust in my true Self. I knew that if I could do that, God would execute the next step in my life perfectly.

The guard, with a look of disgust, turned a huge logbook around. "Sign your f****n' name and get the hell out of here," he snarled.

I took the pen, signed my name, said thank you, and walked out the front door. It was as simple as that. I felt I had walked through the darkness of hell and into the light. Grace had never left me.

I stepped out the door and immediately encountered the Spanish kid's family. They all had gathered on the sidewalk, just as he said they would, anxiously waiting for him to walk through the door and into their arms. My heart ached for all of them, especially for my young friend, knowing that this beautiful reunion would never happen.

[Months later, I heard the price that the young man had paid. He was locked up that same day and shipped back upstate a week later. His work release was revoked. At his parole hearing, the board gave him two more years in prison.]

A few years before that could have been me. I might have blown my chance too. Thanks to the *shakti,* I didn't. Under the same set of circumstances I had made it back to the world, free again after six years, my destiny unfolding with each step.

Once again, my body was free. But more important, *I* was free. I was living the *true* meaning of freedom.

Epilogue

It's now the year 2007 – 21 years since I walked out of prison and back into "the world." I am 68 years old, and my life has been better and more exciting than I ever could have imagined.

I remember going through the front gate of Fulton Correctional Facility headed for a weekend furlough with my family. After serving 6 years, I was given $50.00, a sport jacket that was 3 sizes too big, a pair of pants, 2 pairs of underwear and sweat sox, a pair of tennis sneakers and a pair of shoes. That was it. I had no other money, no place to live and no job, yet I felt totally confident and excited about my future. Although I had nothing else in the world to support me, for the first time in my life I had *me*, and that was all I needed.

The time since has been truly amazing. My everyday experience has been one of an overwhelming abundance of support and acceptance. Everywhere I have gone, doors have opened and I have been welcomed. I never hid the fact that I was a convicted felon. I have always felt confident in speaking openly about it, wherever I have gone, without fear. Suffice it to say that paying attention to my Inner Self guided me to found – and then walk away from – a completely legitimate and spectacularly successful business; to join in partnership with a friend to produce off-Broadway plays; and eventually to realize a true dream of my heart in the form of "Pop Doo-Wop and the Golden Sounds of the Fifties." (That's me and my live show, featuring the great groups from the '50's.) But that's another story for another time.

As much as I enjoyed doing the shows, my heart and soul were always with Siddha Yoga, the ashram, and with Swami Muktananda and his successor, Gurumayi Chidvilasananda. And when Tom Toomey asked me to join the Prison Project in 1987, I became a volunteer Prison Project teacher and began traveling with Tom all over the United States and Canada, doing workshops and programs in prisons, meditation centers and ashrams, offering the ancient teachings of Siddha Yoga, the power of meditation and the wisdom of the guru to thousands of people, both in prison and out, right up to the present. Over the years, I have been in awe as I watched so many wonderful souls receive *shaktipat*, the grace-bestowing power of God. It has been the greatest satisfaction in my life to see the loneliness and fear in their eyes permanently replaced by real freedom and joy, anxiety and tension replaced by contentment and true peace.

And my family? Not long after I was released, Ramona consented to let me see the kids on the weekends. I would pick them up, get on a bus or train, and we would go to different places together: a movie, a restaurant or a friend's apartment in Manhattan. It didn't matter where, just as long as they were with me. Our family was on its way to becoming whole again.

All through this time, my Inner Self kept reminding me that my marriage was over but my love for Ramona was not. Ramona did re-marry, to a great guy who loves and supports her totally. To this day, our relationship has grown so much closer and we trust each other far more then we ever did when we were married. I am even close to her new husband; whenever I am in San Diego, they always invite me to stay at their home with them. Ramona has gone from being a shy, innocent and naïve teenager, when I first met her, to an incredibly dynamic and highly successful business woman. She currently owns a tax preparation center in San Diego with a full staff of employees.

My daughter Alana got married five years ago to a young man I feel is my third son. They own a home in Andover, New Jersey and are now beginning their own family. My oldest son, Adam, who lives in West Palm Beach Florida, just graduated college and plans to open a training center for athletes. My youngest son, Jason, is a great light in our family. He is a waiter at my friend Myron's restaurant in New York, as he works toward a career as a musician. My oldest daughter from my first marriage, Gina, moved to Arizona with my three grandchildren. My oldest granddaughter, Brittany, just gave birth to a perfect little boy, making me a great-grandfather.

When I was released from prison, I made what was to become the most important commitment I have ever made: to make meditation the most significant priority in my life. I vowed to my heart, to my truest Self, to God, that I would begin every day with meditation from that moment on, without fail, without compromise, no matter what life brought me. I would never adjust meditation to my life, but always adjust my life to meditation. I have never broken this commitment. It has been my relentless practice for the past 21 years.

In so doing, I came to understand that I have consciously turned my life over to God, with the result that everything has changed dramatically. I find myself, right up to this very moment, experiencing life with greater abundance than I ever knew existed. I experience incredible strength, conviction, joy and *freedom* – with the precious time to enjoy it all completely.

I want to leave you with what I now know. When I look back on my time in prison and remember the walls, the gun towers, the 15-to-life sentence and all that went with it, I can say – without question – that those six years were the happiest I had ever known. I learned to trust, with absolute certainty, that life knows exactly what it is doing, and always, ALWAYS, acts perfectly. And I continue to receive far more than I could ever give.

It is my intention in writing this book to offer that experience to all of you, my true brothers and sisters everywhere: "Maximum Security and True Freedom."

Acknowledgements

To my Mom and Dad, Jack and Gertrude Gompers. You always gave me your love. I am so grateful! I miss being with you but you are always with me fully in my heart.

To my brother Lou and my sister-in-law Trudy, no matter how it ever looked on the surface, your heart and your love have always been there. I will never forget.

To my daughter Gina. Our hearts know the truth.

To my children, Alana, Adam, Jason, and their mother, Ramona, my great friend and love. What words can I offer to express my gratitude for your unwavering love through all the darkness and pain? You were always there, even when I couldn't touch you. You are this book, you are my life.

To my mentor, my dear friend, Tom Toomey, whose dedication and commitment to his spiritual life, to God, has been a deep inspiration and support on my journey to freedom.

To my dear friend Robert (Murali) Pacini. You were there for me all through my time in prison and you have been there for me, once again, for *Maximum Security*. You are the quintessential open heart and I am so grateful to have you in my life.

To Joey ("Uncle Joey") Brodeur, my heart, my soul buddy, my protector. Thank you for filling my life and giving so much to all of us.

To Howie, Artie, Myron, Ira, Elliot, P-Dub, and Paul Karasik. Through your friendship I have never been alone. You are the ink on these pages.

To Winnie Marucci, wherever you are. My heart still aches from the memories of my insensitivity and indifference toward you at a time in our lives when you needed me most. Can you forgive me?

To Ronnie, my eternal gratitude for your incredible faith and belief in me, but most of all for your love.

To Willie Winfield and Raoul Cita of The Harptones, Earl Lewis, the great lead voice of The Channels, and Bernard (B.J.) Jones, "Mr. Bass Man." It was because of your unselfish support and kind friendship that my career as "Pop Doo-Wop" and my show "The Golden Sounds of the Fifties" was brought into being. How could I ever forget you guys?

To Don K. Reed, who opened the doors for "Pop Doo-Wop" to come into being. You never wanted anything for yourself – you did it just for the love of the music. Thank you, Don!

To Uma Hayes, for your direction, unwavering honesty and directness, so appreciated and necessary in developing this manuscript.

To Jane Freeman, for being my editor and friend. Your belief in *Maximum Security* and in me has been my great fortune.

To Alan Hack, we have a relationship that I greatly honor and respect. You seemed to come out of nowhere and have always surfaced at exactly the perfect moment, for me as well as for this book.

To Catherine Royce, for your courage, strength and so much more that I will *always* hold in my heart.

To my nephew Michael, whom I love and trust and root for, always.

To my former business manager, Manny Schmidt, who has been a perfect gift, whom I respect and admire greatly and who has meant so much to this effort.

To Tony Putman, for your wonderful insight, patience and friendship in supporting *Maximum Security* from the beginning, then re-entering the project when the manuscript was almost complete as the publisher, taking the manuscript and the project to a whole new level. It is perfect that you have come. It has been an amazing gift.

To Lerissa Patrick, for your amazing tolerance and patience, along with your incomparable writing skills, that allowed much of *Maximum Security* to blossom. You taught me the difference between the writings of a speaker and the true expression of an author. It changed everything for me. Your greatness shines forth everywhere in the manuscript.

To Lorena Rostig, whose unwavering faith and energy have been the indispensable ingredients that inspired and propelled *Maximum Security* into being. You came into my life at the exact moment *Maximum Security* and I needed you. Indeed, you were a gift of grace. I could not have done it without you. My deepest gratitude and love go with you always.

To the informer who set me up, the lawyer who misrepresented me, all the people who betrayed me, and all of my life's experiences that initially brought me great pain and fear, I wish to offer my eternal gratitude and respect for the immense love and compassion hidden in your actions, for it was in the intensity of each experience that I was finally able to "wake-up" and see the Truth.

Finally, and above all, thank you to Gurumayi and Baba. Through your endless wisdom, guidance and love, I have come to better understand who you really are, and it is through knowing you that I have found my own true Self.

Index